THE RACE OF THE CENTURY

The Battle to Break the Four-Minute Mile

Also by Neal Bascomb

The Nazi Hunters

Sabotage

The Grand Escape

The Racers

THE RACE OF THE CENTURY

The Battle to Break the Four-Minute Mile

NEAL BASCOMB

SCHOLASTIC
FOCUS
New York

All rights reserved. Published by Scholastic Focus, an imprint of Scholastic Inc., *Publishers since 1920*. SCHOLASTIC, SCHOLASTIC FOCUS, and associated logos are trademarks and/or registered trademarks of Scholastic Inc.

The publisher does not have any control over and does not assume any responsibility for author or third-party websites or their content.

Library of Congress Cataloging-in-Publication Data Available
ISBN 978-1-338-62846-3

10 9 8 7 6 5 4 3 2 1   22 23 24 25 26

Printed in Italy   183
First edition, March 2022

Book design by Keirsten Geise

To those who dare the starting line

Prologue

SEVENTY YEARS AGO, most people considered running four laps of the track in four minutes to be beyond the limits of human speed, foolhardy, and possibly dangerous. A Frenchman asked of the first runner who broke the four-minute mile, "How did he know he would not die?"

But the barrier—physical and psychological—begged to be broken. The figure "seemed so perfectly round," one writer explained: "four laps, four quarter miles, four-point-oh-oh minutes—that it seemed God himself had established it as man's limit." For decades the best middle-distance runners tried and failed. They came within two seconds, but that was as close as they were able to get. Attempt after spirited attempt failed.

Running the mile was considered an art form in itself, requiring a balance of speed and stamina. The person to break the four-minute barrier would have to be fast, highly trained, and so supremely aware of his body that he would cross the finish line just at the point of complete exhaustion.

In August 1952, three young men set out to be first to break the barrier. Wes Santee was a natural athlete, born to run fast. The son of a Kansas ranch hand, he amazed crowds with his talent and basked in the publicity. Then there was John Landy, the Australian who trained harder than anyone else and had the weight of a nation's expectations on his shoulders. Running revealed to Landy a discipline he never knew he had. Finally, there was Roger Bannister, the English medical student for whom the sub-four-minute mile was "a challenge of the human spirit," to which he brought a scientific plan and a magnificent finishing kick.

All three spent a large part of their early twenties struggling for breath and training week after week to the point of collapse. Money was not a factor—they were all amateurs, and the prize for winning a race was usually a token: a watch or a small trophy. The reward was in the effort, in winning, in being the best.

One of the three finally breasted the tape in 3:59.4, but the contest did not end there. The barrier was broken, but the question remained: Who—when they toed the starting line together—would come out on top and run the perfect mile?

CHAPTER 1

ONLY A SCATTERING of people were there to watch the two men in singlets and shorts tear down the straight of the track at Motspur Park athletics stadium. The sole reason Ronnie Williams hadn't folded was because, in his role as pacesetter, all he had to do was set the speed of the time trial that the other runner, Roger Bannister, wanted to hit and maintain it for a lap and a half. Another pacesetter, Chris Chataway, had covered the first half of the three-lap trial. Motspur Park, in South London, was one of the fastest tracks in England, which was why Bannister had chosen it. The surface was typical for the time: a dirt oval topped with a layer of ash cinders recycled from coal-fired electricity plants.

It would be inadequate to describe what Bannister was doing as simply "running." He was eating up the track at a pace of seven yards a second. Journalist Terry O'Connor described his style: "Bannister had terrific grace, a terrific long stride, he seemed to ooze power. It was as if the Greeks had come back and brought him to show you what the true Olympic runner was like." Bannister was tall—six foot one—and long-limbed, with a chest like an engine block and arms that moved like pistons. So balanced and even was his foot placement that some people said he could have walked a tightrope as easily as a track. There was no jarring shift of gears when he accelerated, as he did now, at the end of the three-quarter-mile time trial, only an even increase in tempo. He loved that moment of acceleration at the end of a race when he drew upon the strength of leg, lung, and will to surge ahead.

Bannister shot across the finish, and timekeeper Norris McWhirter punched down the button on his stopwatch. On reading the time, he gasped. Norris and his twin brother, Ross, had been friends with Bannister since their days at Oxford University. Norris had always known there was something special about Bannister, but as he stared down at his stopwatch that July afternoon, he could hardly believe the time: three-quarters of a mile in 2 minutes and 52.9 seconds—four seconds faster than the world record held by the great Swedish miler Arne Andersson.

After catching his breath, Bannister walked over to see what the stopwatch read. Cinders clung to his running spikes. In those days athletic shoes were made of thin leather molded so snugly to the feet that when the laces were drawn tight, you could see the ridges of the toes. The soles were embedded with six or more half-inch steel spikes, for traction.

"Two fifty-two-nine," Norris said.

Bannister was taken aback. The time had to be wrong. "You could have brought a watch we could rely on," he said.

He always ran a three-quarter-mile time trial before a big race to gauge his fitness level and judgment of pace. This one was particularly important because in ten days' time, provided he qualified in the heats, he would be running in the 1,500-meter final at the Helsinki Olympics, a race he had dedicated the past two years to winning. A good time this afternoon would be crucial for his confidence.

Norris was cross at the suggestion that his watch was unreliable and dashed to a telephone booth near the concrete stadium stands. He put a penny in the slot and dialed, and a toneless voice came on the line: "On the third stroke, the time will be 2:32 and 10 seconds—bip—bip—bip. On the third stroke, the time will be 2:32 and 20 seconds—bip—bip—bip." The stopwatch was accurate.

Bannister always considered that being able to run three-quarters of a mile in three minutes meant he was in top racing shape. He was now seven seconds under that benchmark. All his training for the past two years had been focused on reaching his peak at exactly this moment, and he was certain of a very good show at the Helsinki Games.

However, there was a complication Bannister did not yet know about. As a sports journalist, Norris McWhirter kept his ear to the ground, and he had heard that a semifinal had been added to the 1,500-meter contest because of the higher-than-expected number of entrants. Bannister would have to run not just a qualifying heat but also a semifinal before reaching the final.

The four men bundled into Norris's black car and headed back to Central London. As they turned out of the park, Norris finally said, "Roger . . . they put in a semifinal." They all knew what he meant: three races in three days.

Bannister looked out the window, saying nothing. He had trained for two races. Adding another would require a significantly higher level of stamina.

The closer they got to London, the more they could see of the war's destruction—bombed-out buildings that had yet to be bulldozed and rebuilt. When World War II finished in 1945, the British people discovered that while they had survived, they had grim days ahead. Britain owed £3 billion, principally to the United States. Exports had dried up—in large part because half the country's merchant fleet had been sunk. Returning soldiers found rubble where their homes had once stood. There were lines for the most basic staples, and ration books were required—even for children's sweets.

And the blows kept falling. The winter of 1946–47 brought the country to a standstill, with blizzards and power outages. It was so cold that the hands of Big Ben iced up, as if time itself had stopped. The spring brought severe flooding, and the summer's temperatures were scorching. Adding to the misery was a polio scare. To cap it all, on February 6, 1952, London newspapers rolled off the presses with black-bordered pages: The king was dead. Crowds wearing black armbands waited in lines miles long to see King George VI lying in state at Westminster Abbey. A great age had passed.

Even in sport, the country was faltering and had to learn the sour lesson of being a "good loser" in everything from cricket to rugby, boxing, tennis, golf, soccer, and track and field. It looked as though the quintessential English amateur—one who played his sport solely for the enjoyment of the effort—simply couldn't handle the competition. He looked outdated, inadequate, and tired. For a country that considered its sporting prowess symbolic of its place in the world, this was a distressing situation.

To pin the hopes of a nation on the singlet of an athlete seemed to invite disaster, but Britain at that time was desperate to win at something. Roger Bannister was being set up by the press to be the hero of a country in desperate need of one. His friends knew that he was burdened by the fact.

When not on the track, where he looked invincible, Bannister seemed slight in stature. When he was dressed in long pants and a shirt, his sinewed muscles no longer visible, it was his face you noticed. At twenty-three years old, his high cheekbones, fair complexion, and straw-colored hair flopping across his forehead gave him an earnest expression that was boyish when he smiled, although there was a quiet aggression in his eyes, which looked at you as if they were sizing you up.

The second child and first son of Ralph and Alice Bannister, Roger Gilbert Bannister was born on March 23, 1929. His family lived in a modest home in Harrow, a suburb of London. Bannister didn't come from a family with a long athletic tradition, nor one in which it was assumed that he would go to Oxford University, as he did, to study medicine.

His childhood years were spent largely alone: building models, imagining heroic adventures, and dodging neighborhood bullies. When he was ten, his family evacuated to Bath, to escape the Blitz, Nazi Germany's nighttime bombing raids on the cities of England. But no place was safe. One night, while they were taking refuge underneath their basement stairs, an explosion shook the walls, and the roof caved in around them.

Bannister first discovered the joy of running while playing on the beach. "I was startled and frightened," he later wrote of his sudden movement forward in bare feet on sand. "I glanced round uneasily to see if anyone was watching.

A few more steps—self-consciously . . . the earth seemed almost to move with me. I was running now, and a fresh rhythm entered my body."

An awkward and serious-minded twelve-year-old, Bannister had trouble fitting in at his school. He earned the acceptance of his peers by winning the annual cross-country race. Somehow, this seemed to right an imbalance in his life. He was able to pursue his studies, as well as acting, music, and archaeology, without feeling at risk of being an outcast. Possessed of a passion for running, a surfeit of energy, and a preternatural ability to push himself, he won virtually all his races, though he was usually wheezing for breath by the end.

In 1945, Bannister's father took him to see the gutsy English miler Sydney Wooderson take on Arne Andersson. This was the first international track-and-field competition since the war, and London's White City Stadium was bedlam as Andersson narrowly beat Wooderson. "If there was a moment when things began, that was it for me," Bannister said.

At the age of seventeen, he won a scholarship to study medicine at Exeter College, Oxford. Some of his fellow students were as many as eight years older than him, having deferred placement because of the war. A schoolboy among ex-majors and brigadiers, he quickly realized that running was his best chance to distinguish himself.

On a dreary spring day, March 22, 1947, on the very track in White City where he had watched Wooderson compete, Bannister discovered his true gift for running. He stepped to the mark for the Oxford versus Cambridge mile race, feeling the pressure to run well against his university's ancient rival. From the start, he held back, letting others set the pace. After the bell for the final lap, he felt exhausted but was still close enough to the leaders that he was going to finish respectably.

Then, all of a sudden, he was overwhelmed by a feeling that he just had to win. It was instinct, a "crazy desire to overtake the whole field," he later explained. Through a cold high wind on the back straight, he increased the tempo of his stride, and, to the shock of everyone, teammates and competitors alike, he surged past on the outside, pushing through the tape twenty yards ahead of the others in 4:30.8.

It wasn't the time that mattered but rather the rush of passing the field with his long, devouring stride. This was ecstasy, and it was the first time Bannister knew for sure that there was something remarkable in the way he ran—and something remarkable in the feeling that went with it.

Preparations for the Helsinki Olympics began in the autumn of 1950. Bannister's plan was to spend one year competing against the best international middle-distance runners in the world. The following year, he would focus on training to his peak, running in only a few races so as not to dull his edge.

In the spring of 1951, he flew to Philadelphia to compete in the Benjamin Franklin Mile, the premier American event in middle-distance running. He had his mile time down to 4:09.9, a reduction of more than 40 seconds from his first Oxford race three years before. The press fawned over him, commenting on his traveling alone to the event: "No manager, no trainer, no masseur, no friends! He's nuts—or he's good."

In front of 40,000 American sports fans, Bannister crushed the country's two best milers in a time of 4:08.3. The race brought him acclaim back home. Beating the Americans on their own turf earned him the status of a national hero. When he followed with victories at the British Games and the Amateur Athletic Association (AAA, or "three As") Championships, it seemed that track officials and the press were ready to award him the Olympic gold medal right there and then.

Following his own plan, Bannister stopped running mile races at the end of the summer. He felt he had learned all he needed and should now dedicate himself to training. Tired from all the competition, he took a trip to Scotland to hike and sleep under the stars for two weeks. One afternoon, after a swim in a lake, he began to jog around to lose his chill and suddenly found himself running for the sheer exhilaration of it, across the moor and toward the coast. The sky was filled with crimson clouds, and as he ran, a light rain started to fall. With the sun still warming his back, a rainbow appeared in front of him. He seemed to be running toward it. The rhythm of waves breaking against rocks along the coast soothed him, and cool, wet air filled his lungs. Finally, as the sun disappeared from the horizon, he tumbled down a slight hill and rested on his back. He had needed to reconnect to the joy of running, to get away from the tyranny of the track.

Throughout the winter of 1951–52, while continuing to ready for the Olympics, Bannister immersed himself in his first year of training at St. Mary's Hospital in Paddington, learning the basics of taking a patient history and working on the wards. By springtime he had developed his stamina and began speed work on the track. He stuck to his plan, trusting it. As isolating as it was, it had taken him exactly where he wanted to be. Meanwhile, most other athletes trained under the guidance and direction of the British amateur athletic officials.

Everyone, from the head of the AAA to revered newspaper columnists and, by association, his countrymen as well, expected him to bring back the gold medal. Come the Olympic final, he would have an expectant crowd, the rush of competition, two years of dedicated training, the expectation that it was his last race before retirement, and nobody but himself to blame if he lost.

CHAPTER 2

IT SOUNDED LIKE the whole of humankind had come to Finland to witness the opening ceremony of the 1952 Helsinki Olympics. The roar of applause from the stadium reverberated in the narrow concrete tunnel where Wes Santee was waiting in the front row of athletes on the American team. His outfit was a departure from his usual attire of cowboy shirts and jeans. He wore a dark flannel jacket with silver buttons, gray flannel slacks, and a poplin hat. On his feet was a pair of white patent-leather shoes—a far cry from the cowboy boots or track spikes he usually wore. At six foot one, the twenty-year-old University of Kansas sophomore towered over most of those around him. His shoulders were wide, and he bristled with energy. His was a face that lit up easily with a smile. That afternoon of July 19, he was nothing but a bundle of nervous anticipation as he moved toward the tunnel's mouth. Rain streaked across the opening. He peered past it into the stadium, where hundreds of athletes were circling the track, dressed in a kaleidoscope of colors and styles: pink turbans, flower-patterned shirts, green-and-gold blazers, black raincoats, orange hats. Finally, Santee marched through the Marathon Gate into the arena, his head swiveling from side to side as he took in the three-tiered stadium and 70,000 spectators. It was an awesome sight.

After a circuit of the rain-soaked track, he took his spot on the infield for the official opening speeches. Juho Kusti Paasikivi, the president of Finland, stood at the microphone and announced, "I declare the Fifteenth Olympic Games open!" To the sound of trumpets, the Olympic flag with its five interlocking circles was raised on the stadium flagpole, then a twenty-one-gun salute sounded and 2,500 pigeons were released.

Before the last of them soared away, the Olympic torch was brought into the stadium. Pandemonium ensued. The runner carrying the torch was Paavo Nurmi, a national hero in Finland and the godfather of modern track and field. At one time, Nurmi held every record from the 10,000 meters down to the 1,500 meters. Now fifty-five, Nurmi ran around the stadium, the flaming birch torch in his right hand, his stride as graceful and effortless as ever.

Santee stood in the middle of this international gathering of people, watching the Olympic flame, and the strangeness of the scene overwhelmed him. He was a long way from Ashland, Kansas, the farming town where he was raised. If his father had had his way, Santee would still be there, pitching hay, fixing fence posts, and plowing fields.

Most fathers want their sons to have a better life, but David Santee was not one of those fathers. Wes was raised on a cattle and wheat ranch five miles outside of town. It was practically a pioneer's existence, with no running water or electricity. The owner of the ranch, Mr. Molyneux, was more of a father to Wes than David Santee ever was, and enjoyed taking the boy into town to buy him a double-dip ice-cream cone at the drugstore. When he died, Santee's happy childhood came to an abrupt end.

From that point forward he was at his father's mercy and had to do the work of a man on the ranch. His only freedom was running. He ran everywhere. He ran the five miles to school. When he returned in the afternoon, he ran to the fields to help with the plowing or corralling one of the 400 head of cattle. At dusk, the exhausted boy didn't walk home for supper. He ran. Fast. In cowboy boots. He was always voracious at the end of the day.

Santee suffered the brunt of his father's temper, which was dispensed with fists, a rawhide whip, even a hammer once. Some sons of abusive fathers want to become big enough to fight back. Santee wanted to become fast enough to get away.

Very early on, he recognized that he had a gift for running. He was never very good in a sprint, but if the game was to run around the block twice, he always won. In eighth grade, the high school coach came down to evaluate which kids were good at which sports. He threw out a football to see who threw or kicked it the farthest, a basketball to see who made a couple of jump shots. Then he told the kids to run to the grain elevator. Within a few hundred yards, Santee was all alone and knew he had the others whipped. He had run to the grain elevator and back and taken a shower before the others returned.

What had started as fun—running to chase mice or the tractor—and had then become a way to escape from his father's clutches was now a way to excel. Each race he won bolstered his pride. Over the next four years he scorched up tracks throughout Kansas. He won two state mile championships and was targeted by college track recruiters from coast to coast. He had found his way out. When Bill Easton, the University of Kansas track-and-field coach, offered him a scholarship in 1949, Santee accepted. The KU track team was one of the best in the country, thanks to Easton's guidance.

The summer before he left for college, Santee had his last confrontation with his father. One day, while he was digging yet another six-foot-deep hole in the hard ground for an electricity pole, his father started pounding on his back with his fists because he was digging too slowly. That was it. His shirt soaked with sweat and his hands blistered from the work, Santee stormed back to the house, informed his mother he was leaving, and said goodbye to his brother and sister. He moved in with a friend, who had once told him he could stay if things ever got too bad at home, and lived there until college began.

Coach Bill Easton showed Santee how to turn his raw talent into greatness. It had little to do with changing his short, clipped stride, which had become ingrained in his youth—a long stride would have been dangerous on the uneven terrain of the pastures. Santee had the quick arm swing and knee action of a sprinter. But with his native speed, coordination, long legs, strong shoulders, and ability to relax, he was able to sustain this sprinter style over long distances.

Easton was convinced that reshaping Santee's stride into a more classical motion—arms in a long arc, driving to the extreme with his kicking foot—would do more harm than good. Rather, he taught him how to harness his power through training, pace judgment, and focus. Soon even the seniors on his team struggled to keep up with him in practice and competition.

In the spring of 1951, at the Amateur Athletic Union (AAU) Championships, Santee took 17 seconds off the

5,000-meter record in the junior division, and the next day he placed second in the senior division. He earned a spot on an AAU-sponsored tour to Japan and found himself running in Osaka, Sapporo, and Tokyo. There he met the American half-miler Mal Whitfield, who had won two gold medals at the 1948 Olympic Games. Whitfield advised the young miler to keep his toes pointed straight ahead when striding so as not to lose even a quarter inch of distance with each stride. He also taught him that in the mile race, there was time for only one offensive move and one defensive move, so it was of utmost importance to run strategically.

When Santee returned to Kansas, he felt sure that he was ready for more international competition and announced to local reporters, "I want to make the Olympic team and go to Helsinki, Finland." And in his sophomore year, the "sinewy-legged human jet," as one reporter described him, proved that he was already on his way. Some began to compare him to Emil Zátopek, the Czech star who ran everything from the mile to the marathon.

In his sophomore year, Santee lapped his competitors in the two miles, and in cross-country meets he was pulling on his sweats before the other runners had finished. During the indoor season, he set record after record in the mile, leading his team to a host of victories. It was almost too easy. Santee loved racing in front of large crowds, and his talent just barely outmeasured his confidence.

As the holder of national titles in the 1,500 and 5,000 meters, Santee qualified for the Olympic trial in both events. "I just want to make the Olympic team," he told his coach. "Time or race isn't important." On June 27, in front of 42,000 spectators at the Los Angeles Memorial Coliseum, he placed second in the 5,000-meter trial, guaranteeing himself a trip to Helsinki.

The next day, on one of the coldest June days in Los Angeles history, he readied himself for the 1,500-meter trial. A whistle was blown, the race was called, and Santee approached the starting line alongside Bob McMillen and Warren Druetzler, both of whom he was sure he could beat. He was revved to go. Suddenly, two AAU officials grabbed him by his arms, shuffling him off the track before he could protest.

Santee shrugged them off. "What's going on?" Out of the corner of his eye he saw Bill Easton running across the field toward him. The race starter called, "Runners to your mark!" and then the gun fired. Santee watched helplessly as the trial started without him.

Easton finally made it to his side. "Wes, I'm sorry. We've been in a meeting for over an hour. They're saying you're not good enough to run both races, and they won't let you drop out of the 5,000 meters to run the 1,500 meters."

This wasn't right. Only the previous week, Santee had run the third-fastest 1,500-meter time in AAU history, at 3:49.3. Anger welled up in him, and his fists balled. He looked ready to act out his frustration.

Easton pulled him to one side. The coach had the stocky build of a wrestler, and even though he was in his late forties, he looked quite capable of stopping his athlete if necessary. His voice was calm. "They told me you were only twenty— not good enough to run the 5,000 against Zátopek followed up with the 1,500. I told them we don't particularly want to run the 5,000; we want to run the 1,500. Their only response was 'You qualified for that, and you have to stay with it.'"

There was nothing to be done. Easton knew that there was no rule forbidding an athlete from participating in two events. If Santee qualified, he qualified. But the AAU ran the show, and if a rule interfered with what the AAU wanted, they either ignored the rule or changed it. Sure, Santee was going to Helsinki, but his best chance of coming home with a medal was in the 1,500 meters, not in the 5,000 meters.

When Santee arrived in Finland, he was a jumble of excitement, jet lag, hope, aggravation, patriotism, fear, and confusion—a very different cocktail of emotions from what he needed to perform at his best. Santee had a few days to pull himself together for his qualifying heat. His legs had never failed him before, and no matter how unsettled his state of mind, he expected them to see him through once again. He would prove that he deserved to stand side by side with the best runners in the world.

CHAPTER 3

TWENTY MILES OUTSIDE Helsinki, in the Olympic Village in Käpylä, all was quiet. Australian John Landy and three of his teammates, Les Perry, Don MacMillan, and Bob Prentice, were lying in their iron-framed beds when their coach, Percy Cerutty, burst into the room, swinging the door wide and switching on the lights.

"Wake up! You don't need all this sleep!"

At fifty-seven, Cerutty was a short man with a flowing white mane of hair, a goatee, a weathered face, blue eyes, and the kind of voice that could wake the dead when it was raised. It was often raised. While Cerutty scrambled about the room, Landy and the others shielded their eyes from the light.

Earlier that evening, Landy had scaled the fence surrounding the Olympic training arena to get in some extra training, so he was particularly tired. Compared with MacMillan, the miler in the bed next to his, Landy was a small guy, 150 pounds stretched over a narrow five-foot-eleven frame. He had brown eyes and a shag of curly hair. With his quiet voice, he hardly stood out in a room, but he had a strong presence—a reservoir of calm, uncompromising will. He also possessed a deep and infectious laugh and had a lively, well-rounded intelligence.

Landy and his roommates knew they owed their presence in Helsinki mainly to Cerutty—this madcap little man with his strange notions about pushing oneself to the limit. But all Landy needed now was sleep. He had done very well in the six weeks since he'd left Melbourne. In London, he placed second in the British AAA Championship mile—a surprise to himself and everybody else in White City Stadium. He even set a new two-mile record with a time of 8:54, which qualified him for the Olympic 5,000-meter heats as well as the 1,500 meters.

Born on April 12, 1930, Landy had enjoyed a comfortable childhood. His family lived in a gracious five-bedroom house in Malvern East, an upscale suburb a few miles southeast of Melbourne. Along with his two brothers and two sisters, Landy was loved and supported by his parents, who were neither too strict nor too lenient. His father, a disciplined man and well respected in the community, was a successful accountant who served on the Melbourne Cricket Club board. His mother had a great interest in history and literature. The children attended private schools and were encouraged to pursue their own interests.

Young John was more interested in butterfly collecting

than in running. It was only when he was fourteen and entered Geelong Grammar, an elite boarding school outside the city, that he began to distinguish himself in sport. He excelled in the rough-and-tumble Australian rules football, being quick on his feet and a fierce competitor. In the off-season he proved to be pretty good at track-and-field events. In Landy's final year at Geelong, he won the school cross-country, 440-yard, 880-yard, and one-mile track titles—a clean sweep. He then claimed the All Public Schools Mile Championship with a time of 4:43.8.

When he enrolled at the University of Melbourne to take his agricultural science degree, he continued to dabble in running but considered his prospects limited. Playing center halfback in football looked to be the right choice for his undergraduate sporting activities. He liked being part of a team as well. Like many Australian athletes before him who had great potential, he was losing interest in running from a lack of encouragement and insightful training.

At that time, Australia wasn't known for investing either attention or dollars in track and field. Training methods were years behind Europe and America. The country had a long track-and-field tradition, but it was marked by neglect, lackadaisical training, a dearth of talent, and very little international success. Facilities for training and events were lacking as well. Australia, nearly the size of the continental

United States, had only two standard athletic fields—one of those being Olympic Park in Melbourne, Landy's hometown.

It was there that a friend of Landy's, Gordon Hall, approached him after a race to tell him, "You're not fit." Hall suggested that Landy speak to his own coach, Percy Cerutty, who was a fixture at Olympic Park. To find him, all you had to do was listen for his piercing voice.

The two went over to Cerutty, and Hall introduced Landy. Though not exceptionally tall, Landy towered over the diminutive Cerutty, who just stroked his chin and said, "Never heard of you." Cerutty liked to press an athlete's buttons in order to gauge his reaction and strength of will. Landy fell for the bait, commenting that he was really a footballer and just dabbled in running.

This attitude was anathema to Cerutty, who demanded 100 percent commitment from his athletes. The conversation had barely begun and Cerutty was already walking away. He told Landy that if he was interested—seriously interested—in learning how to run, he should come by his house in South Yarra for another talk. They didn't set a date.

Cerutty knew what he was doing: An athlete needed to choose to be taught.

When Landy finally made his way to South Yarra, the two men sat in Cerutty's tiny study, which was crowded with books, cherry-red velvet couches, dumbbells, a decanter of port, a typewriter, and a jumble of papers and magazines. Landy listened as Cerutty expounded on his philosophy, dispelling the notion that Landy would burn out, or worse, harm himself if he trained too much.

The "human organism" is built to handle stress, he said; the body welcomes it. Through continuous effort, superior fitness is guaranteed. Look at the rigorous training of Emil Zátopek or the Swedish runners Arne Andersson and Gunder Hägg. Landy was fired up by Cerutty's ideas and told him that he would train with him. Cerutty gave him a training outline and sent him out on his own, never inquiring as to whether he was following his guidance. And Landy did not feel the need to offer the information himself—the proof was in his performances.

It took three weeks of hard training and a few lessons on running style for him to see results. On January 20, 1951, he dropped his mile time by 6 seconds. Two months later, after upper-body strengthening with dumbbells and hundreds of miles of conditioning work, his time was down another 10 seconds. On May 22, 1951, he ran a 4:16 mile, an extraordinary improvement. For the first time, he thought he might have a shot at the Olympics.

In December 1951, Landy traveled to the seaside town of Portsea, sixty miles southwest of Melbourne, for a ten-day training camp with Cerutty. Each day before breakfast, the men ran the Hall Circuit, a course that threaded through tea trees, up hills, down steep slopes, and across sand dunes.

Sometimes, Cerutty badgered them to go faster, questioning their manhood or dedication—often both. He ridiculed and taunted them mercilessly, particularly Landy, who he thought needed toughening up. Often he shouted encouragements to his runners like "Move your bloody arms . . . Too slow! Too slow! . . . Children could run faster than that!"

Other training sessions were held on a nearby golf course, where Cerutty had his clients charge up hills to practice the kind of energy explosion they would need in a race. They ran up sand dunes for the same reason, an exercise that Landy particularly disliked. He preferred the rhythmic flow of running on flat ground. For resistance training they sprinted along the beach knee-deep in the surf.

When not running, they swam, surfed, or hiked along the coast—they were in constant motion. The exception was when Cerutty gathered them together to deliver a lecture on his Stotan (part Stoic, part Spartan) philosophy. This he peppered with quotes from Plato, Buddha, Jesus, Freud, Einstein, and Saint Francis of Assisi among others. Cerutty stressed the importance of yoga, nonconformity, a diet of oats, the study of nature and animals, and running barefoot to connect with the Earth.

For Landy, the son of an accountant and the product of private schools, this was wild stuff. He laughed off most of it, but there was wisdom in what Cerutty said about training hard. The body had amazing limits that most people never tested—and Cerutty drove Landy to try. He helped bring out a discipline and a focus that the young runner never suspected he had.

Landy took away from this time with Cerutty more than important lessons about running. He also became one of a tightly knit group of friends—among them Les Perry and Don MacMillan as well as three-milers Geoff Warren and Trevor Robbins. The hard training and rustic setting combined to create an environment that brought the athletes together and forged friendships.

The Australian organizers for the Olympics had set 4:10 as the time to beat in order to qualify for the mile in Helsinki. On January 12, 1952, Landy set out to earn his place on the team. He led from the start of the race, held in Melbourne, pushing harder than ever before, but crossed the finish line a second short. He swallowed his disappointment and only a few hours later ran the 3,000 meters in 8:53, breaking the Australian open record. The training at Portsea had increased his endurance but not his speed at shorter distances.

Two weeks later, in Sydney, he beat MacMillan by inches, but again the time was too slow to qualify. By the cutoff date for selection, MacMillan and Landy had both run the qualifying time in the 1,500 meters, but only MacMillan had run the requisite speed for the mile. When the list of sponsored Olympic team members was published in March, Landy's name was missing. But there was a loophole. If Landy could come up with $750, he could join the team.

It was a lot of money—a year's wages for some—but the Geelong Guild Athletic Club rallied to raise it. They held Saturday night dances and "chook raffles" (the prize was a chicken). With a lot of work and good intentions, the club's members raised a good deal of money, but they were still $250 shy. Landy's father made up the difference. His son was going to the Olympics.

At the Olympic Village in Helsinki, Cerutty finally quieted down, and Landy lay back in his bed. He had made great strides in his development and had run well in England, but still he was unsure how he would measure up against the world's best. He was very sensitive to the fact that he owed his Olympic ticket to the generosity of family and friends and felt under pressure to live up to the efforts they had made to get him there in the first place.

With each day he spent on the track, observing the

speed and fluid style of other athletes, his confidence in his ability to compete against them weakened. His coach may have believed that he had the greatest insight into running and training, but Landy suspected that these European and American runners had pretty good ideas of their own. He knew that he would soon find out how good.

CHAPTER 4

RAIN FROM THE night of the opening ceremony had left the redbrick-dust track in the Helsinki Olympic Stadium a soupy mess. During the night, groundskeepers spread petrol around it and lit hundreds of small fires to burn off the water. The smoke billowed into the sky over the stadium, and the acrid smell lingered in the surrounding streets. By dawn on Sunday, July 20, the track was dry. It was then rolled and leveled before the first athletes arrived. Many of those athletes were representing countries that had been at war with one another just a few short years before. Now they milled about the Olympic Village, passing the time between training sessions, meals, and their competitions.

When Santee woke up in his room in the Village, he wasn't sure what he was supposed to do or where he was supposed to be. When was he competing? Against whom? And when could he train? This important information was hard to come by. He was left to fend for himself, a situation that was utterly foreign to him. He was used to his coach telling him when to arrive for practice, who he was competing against, how to run the race, what to eat beforehand.

This management of the details allowed Santee to concentrate on the one thing he had supreme confidence in: his running.

By the day of his qualifying round, he was still in the dark about his race. When he saw Fred Wilt, an alumnus from Indiana University, on the other side of the locker room, he hurried over to him. Wilt, who had competed extensively overseas, would know what he should do. "I really don't know much," Wilt said after Santee told him who was in the heat against him. "Except that Schade guy. He'll probably run a steady, even race. Follow him."

Shortly after that, an Olympic official called Santee to the track for his heat. He jogged into the stadium, feeling only slightly comforted by that one piece of advice from Wilt. At the University of Kansas, he would have gone over the race in detail on the blackboard in Bill Easton's office, Easton indicating lap times to shoot for, how the other runners traditionally ran, and when to move with the pack or ahead of it. Santee felt very overwhelmed. This was the Olympics. He was representing his country, and, perhaps more important, Kansas too. He was expected to do well, but he felt displaced, like he had been blindfolded, led out into a dark field, and left alone to find his way home.

The starting gun fired. Going into the first turn, Santee was in a good position behind the German Herbert Schade, right where he wanted to be. The lap went well: Schade led, and Santee kept back by several runners but stayed close enough. By the third lap, Santee and the German were alone. The others had fallen back on the pace. Halfway through the race, Santee sensed his legs tiring, but he held on to second position. At 3,000 meters, he heard Schade's time called—8:23—and then his own, 2 seconds slower. It was too fast. The best he had run this distance was 8:44, and he was 150 yards ahead of that pace. He began to lose confidence. He couldn't maintain this kind of speed.

What Santee should have known before this point in the race was that Schade was using his heat to show his speed to Czechoslovakia's Emil Zátopek and France's Alain Mimoun, both of whom were in separate heats and would likely prove Schade's stiffest competition in the final. An Olympic record would be broken if Schade continued at this pace—and he meant to continue.

Half a lap later, Santee lost momentum. His arms and legs turned to lead; his chest couldn't bring in enough breath. By 4,000 meters he felt as if he was hardly moving—the sensation was more like running through water than over a track. Runner after runner passed him, and there was nothing he could do about it. He finished at a dismally slow pace, thirteenth overall, in a time of 15:10.4—the worst showing of his career at this distance.

After the race, as he put on his sweatsuit, he was not only physically exhausted but emotionally exhausted as well. He didn't want to speak to anybody. He was embarrassed, wanting to hole up in his room until they flew home. For an athlete who had seldom known defeat, this was agony.

Two days later, John Landy was preparing for his heat in the 1,500-meter race. He did not like his chances. He had failed to qualify for the 5,000 meters, finishing over 30 seconds behind the winner of his heat, Alain Mimoun, in tenth position overall. It was a poor result—but his personal best, achieved in early February, had been only two seconds faster.

For the 1,500 meters, the top four runners would qualify for the semifinal. The eight-man race included the French and Yugoslav champions as well as America's Bob McMillen and Great Britain's Roger Bannister. Landy's best time in the distance (3:52.8) was several seconds slower than his competitors'. In addition, he was much more accustomed to running a mile than 1,500 meters.

Although only 120 yards shorter than the mile, the 1,500 meters was an awkward race. Standard European tracks, Helsinki's included, were 400 meters in length, meaning that runners competed over three and three-quarter laps. Landy disliked the race because, as he later explained,

"There's nothing graceful about it. You don't start where you finish. It's ugly." The split times were difficult to understand, and, given the incomplete first lap, he found it hard to get into his rhythm.

He warmed up with a light jog on the infield, then stepped to the line. Three minutes and 57 seconds later, his Olympic hopes had been dashed. Patrick El Mabrouk came from behind to finish first with a time of 3:55.8, an unexceptional pace. McMillen, Bannister, and the Hungarian Vilmos Tölgyesi followed, in that order, with Landy one second behind in fifth. As he later described it, the last 100 meters of the race were a "mad scramble," but he was too tired in the final straight to overtake Tölgyesi.

Landy was disappointed in himself. He had traveled all this way and had failed to make even the semifinals. He knew the reason too: Since his good runs in England, he had come off his peak—a consequence of incomplete training. However, he refused to wallow. He figured there was a lot he could learn while he was in Helsinki, especially from the athletes who dominated the games, like Emil Zátopek, who won gold in the 5,000-meter final. He made it his job to study the other athletes at the practice track, watching the style of their running as well as their various training methods.

Zátopek fascinated him the most. Percy Cerutty talked

about the Czech runner often, and Les Perry idolized him because of his infamously hard training schedule and his unrivaled record. The thirty-year-old army major was a frightening sight when running: his bony five-foot-eight frame speeding down the track in an unrhythmic mess of arms and legs, his head rolling back and forth, his tongue sticking out, his face contorted. But all the runners knew he was more fit than they were, and Zátopek did not hesitate to remind them of the fact, often midrace. Just as his competitors were gasping for air, the Czech would sometimes consider it a good time for a conversation.

Along with a pack of other devotees, Landy followed the Czech around the track while he jogged forward and backward, talking about running. He spoke almost as fast as he ran, so there was a lot to take in. Zátopek made his running a way of life and believed in training his willpower in small steps, every day. Discipline was the key.

As for style, which he was accused of lacking, he was plainspoken: "I shall learn to have a better style once they start judging races according to their beauty. So long as it's a question of speed then my attention will be directed to seeing how fast I can cover the ground." Zátopek's three gold medals—in the 5,000 meters, 10,000 meters, and the marathon (his first)—proved to Landy that the Czech was on the right track. And Landy liked Zátopek's analytical approach, which was the opposite to Cerutty's—he didn't talk about Eastern philosophy or have wild theories. He had schedules and methods of maintaining the balance between speed and endurance. Landy had the intelligence and independence to understand that while he owed Cerutty credit for his achievements up to that point, his future path led elsewhere.

~

When Roger Bannister made his way down the tunnel into the Olympic stadium on Saturday, July 26, his face was white, his step uncertain. At 4:30 p.m., he would line up against the eleven best middle-distance runners in the world for the 1,500-meter final. His confidence was badly affected by the fact that he had already run two races to qualify.

The past week had brought only restless nights and days. Bannister and his roommates—sprinter Nicolas Stacey, quarter-miler Alan Dick, and three-miler Chris Chataway—had tried to relieve the tension by joking around with one another, but inevitably their thoughts turned to that second when the starting gun would fire and whether they would prove good enough.

The others had finished their events, nobody in triumph and Chataway most disastrously of all by falling during the last lap of the 5,000-meter final. There were two days left in the track-and-field competitions, and Britain had won only a handful of medals, not one of them gold. Nor had a British athlete won gold in any of the other events. The nation had one hope left: Roger Bannister.

But his legs hurt. He hadn't slept soundly in days. And he was plagued with worry. His qualifying round and his semifinal, both run in the previous two days, had been brutal. To avoid the jostling and elbowing of a crowded field, he ran both races in the second and third lanes, adding at least twenty yards to each. The semifinal had been especially taxing because there was a fight to the finish that placed him only four-tenths of a second ahead of Stanislav Jungwirth from Czechoslovakia, who failed to qualify. Usually, Bannister required three or four days of recovery after such a tough race, but he had only twenty-four hours.

The Duke of Edinburgh arrived in the stands for the 1,500-meter event, to the cheering of the crowd. With the eleven others, Bannister approached the starting line. He had prepared his whole athletic career for this moment. The crowd hushed for the gun. Suddenly, they were off. The German Rolf Lamers carried the field through the first 400-meter lap in 57.8 seconds, looking like he might be pacing for his countryman and the favorite to win, Werner Lueg. Throughout this first lap Bannister stayed to the inside. He did not have the energy to battle in the middle of the pack.

Lamers soon faded, and Lueg took the lead, finishing

the second lap at a slower pace, in 2:01.4. Bannister had managed to come up through the field and was running in fifth place. By the bell, Lueg was still leading. He finished 1,200 meters in 3:03, a slow pace given the field's talent. Only three-quarters of a lap to go. In the radio broadcast booth, BBC announcer Harold Abrahams was worried for Bannister, despite the fact that he was in the right position— third—to make a break: "He is not running as well as one would hope. He is looking rather tired."

In the back straight of the last lap, the race heated up. Two hundred meters from the finish, the whole field was nearly sprinting. Olle Åberg of Sweden and then France's Patrick El Mabrouk tried to surge to the top of the pack. Bannister was next. "Bannister is in third position with 180 meters to go," said Abrahams. "Bannister fighting magnificently. Bannister now trying to get into the lead."

This is it, Bannister thought. Although he had suffered nothing but dread since first hearing about the added semifinal, he was in the ideal spot to win the gold. He had managed the jostling field, kept with the pace, and avoided tripping. As he moved into the final turn, now in second place, he called on the full speed of his finishing kick, his most potent weapon. He gave the order to his legs to go. But for the first time in his life, his kick wasn't there. His legs just didn't have the energy.

Josy Barthel from Luxembourg swept by. Then the American, Bob McMillen. Bannister felt drained and helpless, knowing he had lost. "Bannister is fading!" Abrahams called into the microphone. Lueg held strong, stretching his lead by three yards at the end of the turn. Then Barthel struck, delivering the finish Bannister had wanted for himself. The Luxembourger cruised past Lueg in the final 50 meters, with McMillen not far behind. "And it's Barthel wins. Second the American. Third Lueg. Fourth Bannister. Time 3:45.2."

Not even a bronze. Bannister was so exhausted by the end of the race that he had to hold on to the back of Lueg's singlet to stop himself pitching forward onto the track. The British team was distraught. Columnists began to sharpen their pencils. As he headed back to the Olympic Village later that afternoon, fending off the press, who were preparing to excoriate him for his insufficient preparations, Bannister was already looking for a way to overcome what had just happened. He couldn't finish his running career a loser. His answer would be to attempt a challenge that had been in the making for a very long time: the four-minute mile. And he would not be the only one.

CHAPTER 5

ANCIENT OLYMPIC CHAMPIONS were treated like gods—worthy of worship and great odes. In the first Olympic Games, in 776 BCE, the athletes ran naked and barefoot, and the winner, Coroebus, was crowned with a garland made from the leaves and twigs of an olive tree. Before stopwatches, cinder tracks, and world records, athletes measured success by how many victories they had won, and not by their speed. Time was not recorded in those days of sundials and water clocks.

The Romans preferred gladiator fights to athletics, but they made an important contribution to the story of the four-minute mile: They were the first to come up with the measurement. Roman soldiers calculated their long marches in *mille passus* (*mille*: one thousand; *passus*: a two-step stride). Given that each stride was roughly 2 feet 5 inches, the earliest mile translated into roughly 1,611 yards. This was later standardized to 1,760 yards.

By the nineteenth century, "pedestrians," as professional runners were known, were competing on the roads for cash. The mile race was a favorite, and it paid to specialize in that distance. The runners used the milestones on the roads (another relic of ancient Rome) as their starting and finishing points.

The idea of beating a time instead of an opponent evolved gradually. Running a mile in less than five minutes was considered beyond the realm of possibility until Scotsman Captain Robert Barclay Allardice, a famed professional pedestrian, posted a time of 4:50 in 1804, winning 500 guineas for himself in the process. Twenty years later, James Metcalf, "tailor by trade, pedestrian by profession," beat Barclay's time by 20 seconds, and over the next sixty years, milers chipped away at the record, second by painful second.

In 1886, pro runner William Cummings, who had held the record for eight years, faced off against amateur Walter George in what was billed the "Mile of the Century." Twenty-five thousand spectators crowded around a bicycle track to watch George run so fast he left Cummings unconscious behind him on the last lap. His record of 4:12.8 stood for three decades.

In 1915, when American Norman Taber broke Walter George's record by less than two-tenths of a second, it was too slim a difference to warrant much more than a passing remark in the record books. Then, on August 23, 1923, Paavo Nurmi, a twenty-six-year-old Finnish farm engineer, was drawn into a faster first lap than he would have liked by Swedish miler Edvin Wide. Nurmi, who always ran with a stopwatch in his hand, kept up with Wide's fast start. By the third lap, Wide faded, and Nurmi continued the pace, which resulted in his knocking 2 seconds off Taber's record with a 4:10.4. It was a giant step forward, considering how long it had taken Norman Taber to reduce Walter George's mark by just a fraction of a second.

It's not known who first set the challenge of running the mile in less than four minutes, but this barrier became an irresistible challenge to athletes who wanted to guarantee their place in history. When Paavo Nurmi won gold medals at the 1924 Paris Olympics in both the 1,500 and 5,000 meters—*in the space of forty-two minutes*—he seemed capable of anything. Joseph Binks, a noted journalist and former miler, suggested to Nurmi that the four-minute mile was within his grasp, but Nurmi replied, "No! Four minutes four seconds, maybe!" Self-deprecation from the Finn or not, the possibility of a sub-four-minute mile was on the table.

The first miler to run four minutes and single digits was Frenchman Jules Ladoumègue. An orphan who first competed in village-to-village races, Ladoumègue ran on pure emotion. On October 4, 1931, he took advantage of a windless sunny Paris afternoon, and the pacesetting of half-miler René Morel, to reduce the record to 4:09.2.

New Zealander Jack Lovelock was next. On July 15, 1933, in Princeton, New Jersey, he ran a 4:07.6 representing Oxford University. After the race, the *New York Herald Tribune* praised his effort: "It was all so easily accomplished, with so little outward evidence of stress and strain, as to make a sub-four-minute mile seem just around the corner." Lovelock's rival, American Glenn Cunningham, seized the record only eleven months later, with a time of 4:06.8.

In 1937, Sydney Wooderson brought the record back to England. Walter George, now seventy-nine years old, was alive to see it. Wooderson, at five feet six inches and 126 pounds, was an atypical miler. He had the thick glasses and meek demeanor of a solicitor's clerk, but when he set off running, he was a force of indomitable energy. On August 28, 1937, at Motspur Park, pacesetters from his athletic club led him around the first three laps. Then, calling on his famous kick, he handled the last lap alone and registered a time of 4:06.4.

Over the course of three and a half years, between 1942 and 1945, Swedish runners Gunder Hägg and Arne Andersson passed the mile record back and forth between them. Hägg had a more natural, flowing stride, but Andersson trained harder. Their duels inspired great performances. However, the four-minute barrier stood untouched.

Journalists and statisticians were convinced that it was

a barrier that would inevitably be breached. They calculated that the average world-class miler could sustain a speed of 7.33 yards per second (or 15 miles per hour). This meant that the difference between Hägg's best time and the four-minute mile was a short twelve yards—less than 1 percent of the race's total distance. Nothing, the statisticians maintained.

Many wanted the bogey to go away, including the 1912 Olympic 1,500-meter champion, Lieutenant Colonel Arnold Nugent Strode-Jackson, who wrote, "When we stop this nonsense of running . . . with the watch always in mind, we will get back to real racing, the triumph of one runner over another. That is what racing was meant to be and what it will be when we get the four-minute myth out of the way."

Myth or not, the mile barrier remained, and with each passing year, as runners attempted to break it and failed, it grew in fame.

Less than forty-eight hours after the Olympic flame was snuffed out in Helsinki, another competition was held, this one in London's White City Stadium, pitting a British Empire team against the United States. In the 4 × 1 mile relays, Bannister earned the Empire team an early lead, but the second member of his team lost the advantage. Running third leg for the Americans, Santee looked like he would stretch a lead for his team too great to overcome, but Landy, running in the same leg for the Empire team, managed to close on Santee in the final 440 meters.

The anchors—the final runners—for each team traded the lead, but in the end the Americans won. It was the first and only time Bannister, Santee, and Landy competed in the same race. None of the three remembered much about the other two, but as they went their separate ways—Bannister back to life at St. Mary's Hospital, and Landy and Santee on long flights home—they each charted a course in the days that followed that would connect them for many months to come.

Santee flew back with an American team ripe from victory. The US track-and-field team had won fourteen gold medals and thirteen silver and bronze. Santee was one of the minority who did not go home with a medal. Watching the 1,500-meter final, knowing he had beaten the second-place finisher Bob McMillen "every time we had stepped on a track," had left him feeling empty. He was certain he could have won the race if he had been given the chance the AAU officials had denied him in Los Angeles.

Before returning to the University of Kansas, Santee went to visit his parents in Ashland. It was his first trip home since he had left for college. If he hoped his father would say how proud he was of his son, he left disappointed. Back in Lawrence, he sat down with Bill Easton, who had no problem telling his athlete just how proud he was of him. Easton suggested that Santee could learn a great deal from his Olympic experience, but Santee was less philosophical. It was not in his nature to suffer defeat. He wanted to prove that it had been a mistake to prevent him running in the 1,500-meter race, and, more important, he wanted to show how good he really was. So he set his sights on a goal that had always been on his radar: the four-minute mile.

Just days after returning to campus, he marched into the office of the University of Kansas newspaper with an announcement: Wes Santee was going to be the first to run the four-minute mile. For years he had known he was capable. Now his intention was a matter of public record.

Having failed to qualify in either of his events, John Landy was nevertheless excited about the prospect of becoming a faster and stronger runner when he landed back in Melbourne. Emil Zátopek and other European middle-distance runners had given him lessons in how to improve his stride and his training methods to reach a new level. He had also noticed that the European middle-distancers had a smoother, more relaxed stride and ran in spikes that had flat soles and a heel. He wanted nothing more to do with the

Australian kangaroo-hide track shoes that were designed primarily for sprinting on grass tracks and had spikes built up in the front. These made it awkward to lower the heel to the ground and forced the runner to run on their toes. Shoes alone would not change his running style: He would have to practice the arm and leg action of the Europeans until it became habit.

But it was not running style that distinguished Zátopek from every other distance runner in the world. It was his training schedule. If achieving fast mile times was a question of working hard, Landy was ready for it. On the flight back to Australia, he spent many hours rehashing in his notebook the type of training sessions that Zátopek had discussed with him and other runners, and he came up with a plan to achieve for himself the kind of fitness that Zátopek revealed in Helsinki. By doing so, he hoped to beat Don MacMillan's national record in the mile—4:08.9—and win the 1953 Australian Championships.

Of the three runners, Bannister suffered the most for not having lived up to expectations. If it were not for a horse named Foxhunter, whose winning jump came eight minutes before the closing ceremonies began, the British would have gone home without a single gold medal. Track-and-field fans were furious, and Bannister was a lightning rod for most of their criticism. Not only did he have to read in the newspapers about how he had let his country down, he also had to suffer those who stopped him on the street demanding to know what went wrong. This scrutiny was a difficult thing to bear at twenty-three years of age.

Bannister had always thought that he had a "greater degree of self-determination" than others, but the Olympics had rudely disabused him of this notion. He was human, just like everybody else. Ridiculed and defeated, he decided that only an ambition greater than an Olympic gold could absolve him of what had happened in Helsinki. He couldn't simply retire from running after suffering such a defeat. He wanted to silence his critics with an achievement most thought impossible: the four-minute mile. Then they would know what kind of athlete he was.

CHAPTER 6

WEARING FLAT-SOLED SAND shoes, John Landy was running around a bluestone gravel path in Melbourne's Central Park, watching his shadow. He might never catch it, but he could learn from it. He studied the rhythm of his legs and the movement of his arms, and, over the course of his run, he balanced the action of both. The higher he carried his arms, the more distance he won from his stride. If he overextended, he lost equilibrium in his stride and wasted energy.

The technique he was developing was more complicated than simply swinging his arms out and up as far as possible. Rather, he was looking for symmetry of form: the place where his arm action was completely in sync with his knee lift and the drive from his hips. His head needed to remain level, his center of gravity still, his shoulder muscles relaxed, and his feet landing from heel to toe, nearly flat-footed. And all of this needed to occur effortlessly. Slowly he was shaping his running style into one that made it look like he was floating over the track.

Cerutty had promoted a low arm carriage, believing that

man should run like a rooster, clawing at the air. Landy preferred to copy the European runners, who had proven themselves superior in style and performance at Helsinki. "They don't run on their toes like sprinters and paw the track with their spikes as I used to," Landy said. "With a higher arm carriage your knees automatically lift and you get a slightly longer stride. But, most important, there is no tension in the leg muscles. When it comes to the final spurt you have so much extra strength to get on your toes and sprint home." With each passing day, his body grew more accustomed to this new style, and he was getting more return for his effort.

He wanted never to step to the starting line again unless he was the fittest person on the track. His training sessions required intense dedication, and they were run smarter and harder than any guided by Cerutty, who had his gang run until they hurt and then pushed them further. Running a fast mile required more than simply putting up with pain. According to Zátopek, one had to train for speed. Improvement there was won by subjecting the body to periods of high stress at a fast pace while reducing the recovery time between these periods.

Landy's agricultural-science studies demanded that he train at night, after he had finished with his papers and reading. At eleven o'clock or past midnight he slipped quietly out of the house, making sure not to wake his parents or four siblings, who had little idea of the extreme effort he was making. Many nights it was difficult to force himself to put on his shoes and get out there. He often figured that he was too tired and that he might be better off leaving his run until the next day. Or that he deserved a day off. But he would convince himself to run at least a few laps. "It's like a car starting. There's an immense amount of energy you need to start the car, but once you're rolling, it's easy." Since returning from the Olympics, he hadn't missed a single training session.

On a typical night, he ran a series of alternating fast and slow laps around the 600-yard gravel path in Central Park. The only sound his footsteps hitting gravel, he concentrated solely on how much faster he could push himself. He didn't carry a watch: His effort was measured by the interplay of exhaustion and recovery. For most of the lap, he would maintain a fast even pace—but not an all-out effort. Then he would burst ahead and sprint until his legs felt unsteady. Next he would reduce his pace to a jog, feeling his breath return and the pain ebb. By stressing his legs and lungs to such an extreme point, he was immunizing himself to the pain.

An hour and a half into the session, Landy had usually run between eight and twelve 600-yard laps at a pace of roughly 90 seconds each (the equivalent of a 65-second

440-yard lap). Between each, he jogged a lap of the oval path in four minutes. He repeated these sessions five nights a week. On the remaining two nights, he ran seven miles, sometimes more, at a pace between five and a half and six minutes per mile, along the roads leading out of Melbourne. This was to build endurance.

Long after midnight he returned home, took a shower, and collapsed into bed. His resolve was extraordinary, and it was sustained by a still-developing attraction to running. It was quite unlike playing football with a team: How well he ran the mile was entirely up to him. And the harder he trained, the more mastery he had.

Each day, at the University of Melbourne, he attended lectures on subjects like soil science, bacteriology, and farm economics. In the evenings, he returned to Malvern East to have dinner with his family. Except for drinking a great deal of milk, his diet was completely normal. He would relax for a spell after dinner, then withdraw to his room to study for several hours before going out to train.

In October, Les Perry returned from his Scandinavian tour. Perry had probably seen Landy run more than any other person, and he knew how much his friend had improved under Cerutty. But when he visited him at Central Park, Perry was astounded. Landy's legs and arms were more defined. His running style had been transformed. And his speed . . . Perry tried to keep up with him on several laps, but he couldn't.

He knew Landy had been disappointed in Helsinki, that it was in his nature to try to right the wrong of not performing at the level some might have expected, but this kind of speed and repetition work was beyond his imagination. "I've had a bit of a routine," Landy admitted, and told Perry he had been following Zátopek's advice. Perry suspected that the Australian track-and-field community, Cerutty included, were in for a surprise when Landy next took to the track.

In the history of athletics, the best way to train, for how long, and at what intensity was often a matter of experimentation. Ancient Greek athletes skipped, jogged, hopped, and sprinted, occasionally while rolling a large hoop in front of them. They understood the importance of increasing exertion over time; wrestler Milo of Croton walked every day with a calf in his arms, gaining strength slowly in his arms and legs as the calf grew bigger.

The ancient Romans had their own methods. Athletes' diets were limited at first to dried figs, boiled grain, and fresh cheese, with meat being gradually introduced later. To get used to pain, they had their slaves flagellate their backs with rhododendron branches. They took tepid baths and slept a lot, which was supposed to promote muscular strength.

The famous miler Captain Barclay set down his ideas in writing in 1813, and generations of "pedestrians" followed his advice. Some of his suggestions, like purging the body with Glauber's salt, eating a breakfast of "beef-steak or muttonchops underdone, with stale bread and old beer," and lying in bed naked for a half hour after exercise, were nonsensical. However, he also advised a rigorous regime of exercise. It had worked for him, so others suspected they would benefit from his methods as well.

Up until the nineteenth century, it was widely believed that too much exercise guaranteed nothing more than an early death. Doctors thought the heart had a fixed number of beats in a lifetime and that speeding up the heart rate during exercise was a foolish waste of a precious resource.

That athletes persisted in their efforts to see what was physically possible was testament to humankind's innate tenacity and its desire to succeed. Walter George's training methods included speed drills, running on the spot—on his toes—and long walks. In 1910, Alf Shrubb was walking sixteen miles a day, three or four times a week. And in the late 1920s, marathoner Arthur Newton recommended sessions of twenty miles a day.

Jack Lovelock believed that while hard work was

necessary, an athlete risked getting "stale" if he ran too many races. He espoused "peak training": building up his stamina, then doing speed work, and saving the best for race day. In the 1930s, German physiologist Woldemar Gerschler promoted "interval training," advising athletes to run one fast lap on the track followed by one slow one. These were timed to ensure strict routine. Zátopek came up with the same idea by himself but refused to time his runs.

Meanwhile, the Swedes, led by Gunder Hägg, believed that the key to training lay in "speed-play," which they called *fartlek*. This also involved fast and slow combinations of running, but away from the track. The thinking was that athletes needed to experience the joy and freedom of running through forests and up and down hills, judging for themselves when to accelerate and when to hold back. The track was for races.

Throughout the development of new techniques, doctors and laypeople alike continued to advise against the perils of so much running. In 1927, British physiologist Archibald Hill wrote that "it's not unusual for an athlete to tear a tendon, or to strain a muscle, and not unknown even for him to pull off a piece of a bone by an exceedingly violent effort. We are obviously not far from our limit of safety. If we doubled our speed of movement . . . athletics would become a highly dangerous pastime." Despite studies proving otherwise, the general belief was that overtraining could permanently damage the heart and other essential organs. Yet athletes continued to push to improve.

Training had evolved a long way from carrying calves and flogging backs, but not to the point of certainty. By the 1950s, coaches and former athletes had started a cottage industry out of giving (often conflicting) advice. Fads were common, and the latest champions were proclaimed to have the perfect method—until they were beaten by others. The only sure thing was that every athlete had to find their own way.

Landy had found his own way since returning from Helsinki, and he followed it mercilessly. His new running style and Zátopek-inspired routine promised great returns, and until the start of the Australian season he had no way of knowing how great these would be. When Saturday, October 25, 1952, arrived, and with it the first race of the outdoor season between Victoria's amateur athletic clubs, ten weeks had passed for Landy without a race or even a timed trial. But he had run over 500 miles in training—many at near race pace.

He knew he was running well against his friends on the gravel path at Central Park but had no idea what the clock would say. In the event, he crossed the finish line in the mile race in 4:17. His nearest competitor was over 100 yards behind. The Melbourne *Argus* reporter Ken Moses believed that Landy had held back and that he could have run at least 5 seconds faster. Moses predicted that Landy would break Don MacMillan's Australian mile record of 4:08.9 by the end of the season.

The following week, Landy ran a three-mile race, beating the Australian cross-country champion Neil Robbins by 300 yards and trimming Les Perry's record by 16 seconds. It was clear that he was on the verge of something extraordinary. On November 15, in the mile at Olympic Park, he led from the middle of the first lap and finished half a lap ahead of his competitors in 4:14.8.

After the race, Landy entertained questions from the small herd of Melbourne athletics reporters. "Two- and three-mile events are my objective at the moment," he said. "I am out to build up stamina and only racing in those events will help me. It was stamina that beat me when I was away at the Games, and I do not want it to happen again."

On December 12, Landy attended a reunion of Australian Olympians held at runner Bob Prentice's house. It was a Friday night, a chance to let off some steam, take a break from training, and relax with friends. The guests drank Foster's lager, ate sausage rolls, and reminisced about Zátopek and the other sports stars they had met. They avoided talking about their defeats at the hands of the much more capable European and American runners.

The next day brought a welcome break from a week-long summer storm that had flooded highways throughout Victoria. Landy decided to get some fresh air and walk to Olympic Park. His race wasn't until half past two.

On his way he stopped for a chocolate ice-cream sundae. When that failed to satisfy his appetite, he ate a couple of meat pies to hold him over until after the race. Then he strolled along the banks of the Yarra River for a few kilometers until he got to the stadium. Olympic Park was set within a natural bowl surrounded by grass-covered hills on three sides and concrete tiers of seats on the fourth. Its track was made of crushed scoria, a porous rock cinder produced from volcanic eruptions. At best the place was unremarkable, and, despite its name, it had never hosted an Olympics.

By two o'clock, Landy had switched into his Geelong Guild singlet and the white European track shoes he had brought back with him from Helsinki. He warmed up: a few stretches, some jogging, a couple of sprints. In the back of his mind he thought he might have a fast run in him, but he planned to wait until halfway through the race to decide whether or not he would make an all-out effort. It would depend on his rhythm and how he was feeling in the moment. There was no sense going into the race weighed down by the expectation of a fast time.

The stands were lightly scattered with family and friends, including Landy's parents. Many of the spectators chose to sit on the hill along the finishing straight, where they spread wool rugs on the grass and sipped from flasks of cordial or tea. The meet, as was typical for Australia, felt like a country picnic.

"On your marks . . . set . . ." The starter's gun fired. Les Perry went out fast—faster than normal. Without Landy knowing about it, Perry had decided to pull his friend around the track for as long as he could. A sixty-second lap was flat-out sprinting for him, and three-quarters of the way through the first lap he was still in the lead but fading. As Landy passed him on the straight before the end of the first lap, Perry whispered to himself, "Do it, John," hoping that his friend would break Don MacMillan's record.

Landy was now on his own. He finished a very good first lap in 59.2 seconds. Running easily and relaxed, despite the blistering pace, he completed the half mile in 2:01. For the past ten weeks he had run countless laps at a hard pace and was nearly immune to the pain caused from exertion. The bell rang for the final lap, and the timekeeper shouted out, "Three minutes 3 seconds." His time would be good—at least good enough to break MacMillan's record. He felt he had a fair bit of acceleration left in his legs. "Then," he said later, "I went."

The crowd of 200 people rose and cheered as Landy entered the back straight. He increased his tempo but maintained rhythm, pressing harder and harder. When he passed the 1,500-meter mark in a little over 3:45, his friends shouted themselves hoarse. In full stride, he broke the tape and slowed to a jog. His breath was heavy, but he was nowhere near the point of collapse.

Within moments, reporters crowded around. Then the loudspeakers announced the time: 4:02.1. The third-fastest mile in history. Everyone in Olympic Park gave him a standing ovation, and reporters' pencils flew across notebooks. Landy had brought his best mile time down by eight seconds and had approached Gunder Hägg's long-standing world record to within seven-tenths of a second. He told the reporters about his new running style and said that for the first time in his athletic career, he had the confidence in his conditioning to lead from the front. "Most of the credit must go to Perce [Cerutty]," Landy said. "Had it not been for him I would not have got anywhere near my time today. Only hard work gets results. Perce has been telling us that all the time, and our trip to the Games confirmed what he said."

After Landy signed the necessary forms to ratify the

record, he celebrated with his friends over some beers. It had been the most unexpected and therefore the most rewarding race of his life. He was overjoyed.

His 4:02.1 run changed everything. Winning the Australian Championships and breaking the Australian mile record were minor in comparison to what was possible now—and to what was expected of him. From the most unlikely of places, by the most unlikely of athletes, the world was put on notice that the four-minute-mile barrier was within range.

CHAPTER 7

IT WAS THE McWhirters who telephoned Bannister to tell him the news. They had just seen the new issue of *L'Équipe*, the Parisian sports paper that picked up all the international newswires. "The Australian, John Landy, just ran 4:02.1," Norris McWhirter said. Bannister was stunned. He had met Landy in England and had run against him in the first round of the 1,500 meters in Helsinki. Certainly he was no 4:02.1 miler back then. This kind of progress was difficult to imagine.

He wasn't alone in his disbelief. Newspaper sportswriters doubted that a miler who failed to qualify for the 1,500-meter Olympics final could have dropped 8 seconds from his best mile in the span of a few months. Arthur Daley of the *New York Times* wrote, "[Landy is] either one of the seven wonders of the age or something's wrong somewhere. It would indeed be nice to hear that Landy's 4:02.1 is a completely legitimate performance. For the present, please pass the salt." Three weeks later, when Landy clocked a 4:02.8 in a stiff wind, mea culpas were offered by his doubters, Daley included.

How well the Australian miler was running was far from being Bannister's only concern at that time. Studying medicine took a gargantuan effort. Doing so while trying to accomplish the impossible in athletics would have been asking too much for most people, but not for Bannister. His days started in his basement apartment in Earl's Court, where he lived a self-described "chaotic" existence, cooking for himself (usually a quick meat stew or pickled herring for protein) and trying to find spare moments for laundry and chores before heading to St. Mary's Hospital in Paddington. To study at the small teaching hospital, Bannister had won the scholarship established by its dean, Lord Moran, Winston Churchill's doctor. Moran was known for recruiting athletes because he believed that sport taught character and made for good doctors.

During lunch—his only break in a day of making rounds, studying, and writing papers—Bannister hurried from the hospital and took the London Underground two stops to Warwick Road. After a quick walk to Paddington Recreation Ground, he paid his sixpence, changed into his running gear, and within a few minutes was doing fast laps. There was no time to waste with stretches and jogging. He trained for thirty-five minutes before showering, grabbing a bite to eat, and returning to the hospital.

His failure in Helsinki had left him with a need to

redeem himself. With a year and a half left of medical studies, his running days were numbered, and he knew that an Olympic gold was simply never going to be his. But the more he thought about the mile barrier, the more he recognized its significance. Until broken, it would stand as a limit to human endeavor. And the defeated Olympian in him wanted to be the one to break it first.

Since Landy burst onto the international scene with his 4:02.1 mile, Bannister had stepped up his training. He trained alone and without a coach, convinced that he was the only person who could get the best out of himself. Like Landy, he preferred to train at night, mostly on the cricket field at Harrow School near his home. He would jump over the fence into the school grounds, then set off. The fifteen acres of fields and hills gave him the freedom to run at will.

In the darkness, with the trees and other static objects hidden from sight, he had the feeling that his running had no measure other than the energy exerted. But the darkness was not without perils. The year before, he had run into some concrete blocks left in the grass and gashed his leg down to the bone. Only after climbing back over the fence and flagging down a car was he able to get to a hospital.

Nonetheless, these sessions were exhilarating. They were best described as fartlek: Sometimes he ran fast, sometimes slow, up hills, down slopes, judging for himself when to force his legs and when to hold back. After twenty minutes he had usually worked himself up to a peak where he was running 800 yards at near maximum speed. When he ascended hills, he focused on gaining strength in his legs; when descending, he focused on his balance. Some nights the sessions were so hard that it took several days to recover. Other nights he held back.

By early March he was ready for the track. To continue to improve his fitness while balancing his studies, he needed to get more from his training. Each day was a test against the previous one. In one session he ran ten laps at 63 seconds each with only two or three minutes' rest in between. Although the track work stole the joy from running for him, he was fascinated by the daily adjustments in speed and effort that he made to get the most from his body.

Few had examined the human body's capacity to withstand punishment as closely as Roger Bannister. In addition to the grueling life of a medical student and the rigors of hard-core athletic training, he had a third job: finishing his research scholarship at Merton College, Oxford, where he was investigating the physiological effects of running. In March 1953, he was preparing two papers: "The Carbon Dioxide Stimulus to Breathing in Severe Exercise" and "The Effects on the Respiration and Performance during

Exercise of Adding Oxygen to the Inspired Air." Atypical expertise for the average miler.

Bannister's experiments had produced a flood of data on lactate counts, carbon dioxide readings, and oxygen consumption levels. In the two and a half years since beginning the postgraduate research project, he had learned as much about the impact of exercise on the body as it was possible to know. This knowledge came at the expense of a lot of sweat, and blood, from test subjects as well as from Bannister himself.

"Do you think you could come along and help me with an experiment?" he asked Norris McWhirter. Without much reflection or investigation, McWhirter replied, "Oh, yes." He found himself in a small room crowded with a motorized treadmill and a frightening array of attachments: gas bags, meters, valves, pipes, tubes, and pumps. Stripped down to shorts and running shoes, McWhirter winced as the assistant took his hand and drew some blood for a reading.

Then he stepped onto the treadmill and secured his mouth around a rubber tube. Through this mouthpiece, he would inhale oxygen-enriched air and exhale waste air, which would then be analyzed. The experiment measured the effect that different concentrations of oxygen (from a normal level of 21 percent to as much as 75 percent) had on the body as it was running to exhaustion.

Wearing a white lab coat, Bannister fired up the "diabolical machine," as McWhirter referred to the treadmill, and McWhirter began to run up a very steep gradient. Wooden bars to his left and right kept him from pitching over the side, and an electric fan stopped him overheating.

After a couple of minutes, McWhirter was not only exhausted but in pain as well. Granted, he wasn't a distance runner, but the treadmill's speed and gradient were ridiculously harsh. Also, he was running with a rubber mouthpiece attached to his face and a lab assistant repeatedly taking his hand midstride to draw more blood.

Five minutes into the experiment, McWhirter was out of breath, his legs felt like they were buckling, and he experienced what one runner called the "black waves of nausea" caused by too much effort. At six minutes he was finished. His spine went to rubber, his chin fell to his chest, and his knees went up to his face. He was shot off the back of the treadmill into a pile of blankets, in a state of total collapse, barely able to lift his head. The assistant set upon him one last time for a blood sample.

Breathless and splattered with blood, McWhirter finally pulled himself back together after ten minutes. He had three more similar sessions to endure. Bannister had put himself through this same experiment on fifteen separate occasions, managing to stay on the machine for at least three times as long as his other subjects, but all the same driving himself to collapse over and over again.

Afterward, in the laboratory, he analyzed the exhaled gas to see what elements influenced breathing during exertion. A distance runner was limited by their ability to take in and then use oxygen, and this limit could be extended through training. Once the body was suffering from a lack of oxygen, the muscles stopped using oxygen for energy and switched to a mechanism that could be sustained only for a short window of time and that caused the release of lactic acid into the bloodstream. When too much lactic acid was present, it resulted in withering pain and caused muscle contractions.

Since oxygen was the key, Bannister set himself two goals: first, reducing the amount of oxygen he consumed by eliminating unnecessary movements and running at an even pace, and, second, increasing the efficiency of his uptake, delivery, and use of oxygen. He had long since perfected his stride so his movements were neither wasted nor restricted by tension. To keep his head poised and level, he trained himself to look at a point fifteen yards ahead on the track. To maintain evenness of stride, he practiced accelerating while staying relaxed. This was critical. More energy was used in running laps of 58, 62, 64, and 66 seconds than four laps of 60 seconds each. The difference was slight, but it was essential when attempting to break a record separated by a few strides.

For the second goal, improving the uptake of oxygen, Bannister knew that his body was already functioning at a level equaled by few: from his inhalation of air to the lungs' diffusion of oxygen into his blood, to his heart pumping into the capillaries of his legs, to the cells in his muscles converting digested food and oxygen into energy, to the firing of his muscles, to the elimination of the by-products of all these reactions. In 1953, he had a resting heart rate of fifty beats per minute—twenty-two beats lower than the average human. His lungs absorbed 5.25 quarts of oxygen a minute—twice the standard rate. In other words, when he ran, his body was operating nearly 50 percent more efficiently.

But the capacities of his lungs, heart, and muscles were almost fully extended. With every passing year his training reaped diminishing returns. To improve his mile time, he needed to focus his training exclusively on the demands of running one mile and no more. The fartlek training had increased the stamina he needed for the distance, which was mostly a factor of how much oxygen he could take in and put to use. At the Paddington track, he worked on his speed, which at a certain point was about fighting against the body's oxygen limits. Pushing through the tape in less than four minutes demanded balancing and utilizing both types of energy to their breaking points.

From what Bannister understood, which was much more than most, the body was capable of a sub-four-minute mile. With his research and his running experience, taken together, he was able to dissect the way the race needed to be run, not only in terms of training but also in manner and style.

When he fell into bed at the end of a typical day, Bannister had cared for the patients on his ward, puzzled over case histories, attended lectures, crammed two hours' worth of effort into a thirty-five-minute workout, worked on his research project, fulfilled his duties as secretary of the medical society, and led a busy social life that included attending dances, like the Achilles Club Ball, acting as Lord Darlington in Oscar Wilde's *Lady Windermere's Fan*, and enjoying drinks with friends. Roger Bannister was nothing if not a well-rounded man.

CHAPTER 8

TEN THOUSAND PEOPLE were crammed into the stands at Drake Stadium, Des Moines, Iowa, for the 1953 Drake University Relays, many of them waving placards to support their favorite athlete or team. Santee was all set to anchor the distance medley (440 meters, 880 meters, 1,320 meters, and the mile), which was in progress around the track.

His team, the Kansas Jayhawks, had fallen behind Georgetown. Again. "Coach, let's drop out," Santee shouted over the cheering fans.

"Oh, no, no," Bill Easton replied, clipboard in hand. Easton was a commanding presence during a track meet, like a general on the field of battle. "We can't do that. No way."

"I'm going to be too far behind. It's silly for me to just run."

Easton shook his head. "No. I don't want to drop out. We're at Drake."

Santee stepped away. What was the point in wasting energy if they had no chance of winning? As he watched his team slip farther back in the race, his frustration grew. He was sick of taking the baton seventy or eighty yards back and trying in vain to win. This was his third race in nearly twenty-four hours, and all he wanted to do was focus on the open mile.

With the third leg of the medley in progress, Santee again approached Easton on the side of the track. "Come on, Coach. Let's drop."

"No," Easton said, barely even glancing at him. "You're going to run."

Santee walked away and positioned himself for the handoff from Lloyd Koby. Georgetown's anchor, Charlie Capozzoli, had already sprinted away. Santee waited. And waited. And waited. Finally, Koby approached, and Santee began running. They exchanged the baton, and Santee settled in for the mile run. With Capozzoli over half a lap in the lead and striding well, there was no way Santee was going to catch him. He did the best he could and came in in second place, 100 yards behind Georgetown.

Then he stormed off, anxious to avoid a repeat of the previous day's humiliation when Capozzoli had shaken his hand and said, "Hi ya, ya bum." As he passed his coach, Easton called for him to stop. "I don't want to talk to you," Santee said, over his shoulder. His teammates and a host of others watched, astonished, as he strode away.

It was April, the height of the outdoor track season, and Santee was in the best shape of his running career. The previous month, at the Texas Relays, he had run his fastest mile to date—4:06.7—in the anchor leg of the four-mile relay, setting a new record in the event. After leading his team to triumph in the sprint medley, the distance medley, and the two-mile relay, he was named the meet's outstanding performer. Whispers that he was the one to claim the mile record quickly strengthened into downright statements of fact.

At twenty-one, Santee was young for a middle-distance runner—most peaked at twenty-four or twenty-five years of age—but he had tongues wagging about his potential. After the Texas Relays, a *New York Herald Tribune* reporter wrote, "It was a season-launching performance that has never been surpassed . . . Any day, now, they'll be expecting Santee to go for the four-minute mile."

Weekend after weekend, however, his coach neglected to give him the opportunity. Santee understood that winning track meets wasn't an individual affair. Usually he was the loudest supporter on the sidelines, rooting for his Jayhawks. He certainly contributed to their success, running in nearly every distance event. But four races a week was wearing him down. When was he going to be able to concentrate on the mile?

He was churning this question around in his head, pacing the locker room, when his teammates entered. They told him that Easton wanted him to put his spikes back on and go out and race. "I don't want to run with you guys. None of you want to do better," Santee said bitterly. They were shocked. Santee had never refused a race or complained about their performances before. And they couldn't believe he was saying no to Easton. Coach's word was law.

Speechless, they filed out of the locker room and returned to Easton to tell him. Easton stuck his hands in his jacket pockets and with a no-nonsense expression said, "Go get him to run." With only a few minutes before the mile relay was to begin, they pleaded with Santee. He had calmed down enough to realize that he was playing with fire by disobeying Easton. Also, he had a strong sense of loyalty to his team. If they promised to start running with all their heart, he told them, he would run. They agreed.

Back on the track, Easton was cool with Santee. They barely looked at each other, and the coach's only words to him were that he was to run in the third leg. When Santee was handed the baton, he channeled his frustration into a scorching 440-yard lap of 47.4—fast enough to give his anchor, Don Smith, the lead to take home the win for the Kansas Jayhawks.

After the race, Easton told him, "We need to talk."

Bill Easton kept his athletes under constant watch. He knew when they had given a full effort, when one of them had been out too late the night before, and when someone had eaten the wrong kind of food (especially their favorite doughnuts from Joe's Bakery). Nothing got past him. When he asked what the problem was, it was wise to tell the truth.

Santee had a tight routine at the University of Kansas. He usually woke at 6:00 a.m., and was out of his room at the Acacia fraternity house a few minutes after that. The hour-long stroll along tree-lined footpaths and past rustic stone buildings was a pleasant way to get his blood going. He reported for work at the Pi Phi sorority house, where he laid out breakfast for the students—a job that supplemented his athletic scholarship. By eight o'clock he was in class, fulfilling the requirements for his physical-education degree. At lunchtime, he returned to the sorority house, where he bused dishes. Afterward he attended another class before heading down to Memorial Stadium to begin the day's training session, which usually lasted between two and four hours.

On Mondays, the athletes warmed up with a five- to six-mile cross-country run along dirt roads. There was an occasional hill, but mostly it was flat land that stretched for miles, perfect for farming—and long-distance running. The pace was about 50 percent of top effort, which was heated up with quarter- or half-mile dashes. When they returned to the stadium, they changed into fresh singlets and swapped their flat shoes for spikes. Then Easton had them immediately do a quarter mile as fast as possible. He believed that if a distance man had a good quarter-mile time, he could run any event. After a short rest they ran wind sprints barefoot on the grass infield—usually twenty 100-yard dashes.

On Tuesdays they warmed up with a two-mile cross-country run, then came back for track work, which normally included step-downs from a mile to three-quarters, to half, to a quarter, then back up again, jogging between each. On Wednesdays they ran two miles cross-country and then alternated between fast half miles followed by sprints and step-downs again (but over shorter distances—from a half mile to 600 yards to a quarter mile to 220 yards). On Thursdays they concentrated on speed work, usually eight quarter miles or twelve to sixteen 220 yards. On Fridays and Saturdays they raced. Finally, on Sundays, the team got together for a fifteen-mile endurance workout, easing out the strains and tension caused by racing.

After his training session ended, Santee hightailed it back to the sorority house to serve formal dinner. Then he grabbed some food for himself and returned to the stadium to clean the locker room—another scholarship obligation. By eight o'clock he was back in Acacia House for two hours' study before bed. Opportunities to see his girlfriend, Danna Denning, were usually limited.

They had met the year before at the football stadium, where Santee was selling programs. After Helsinki, he took Danna out on a "Coke date" to test the waters. They went to the Rock Chalk Café, a block from his fraternity house, for a soda and a half hour of conversation before she had to return to her sorority house for the 10:30 p.m. curfew.

In many ways the two were polar opposites. Danna came from a wealthy, established family in Elkhart, Kansas, and had entered KU at the age of fifteen. She cared more about her studies in accounting than sport and was as much an introvert as Wes was an extrovert. While Santee had to work for spending money, she had a generous allowance and drove around in an Austin-Healey her father had given her.

But what they had together worked. One date turned into two and then many. They went to church on Sundays and attended formals together, and Danna would stop by the track to watch him train. By April 1953, talk of marriage and having children was on the table.

Easton frowned on his athletes getting too serious with their girlfriends, but Wes had been able to get close to Danna without losing focus on his sport—not that he had much spare time to lose focus.

A month after Santee's return from Helsinki, the cross-country season began, and he traveled throughout the Midwest for dual meets and championships. The Jayhawks strung together six meet victories in a row. Easton motivated his team with slogans like "KU against the world," but his boys were far from underdogs, with Santee winning every three-mile race he entered.

This was his life. Easton was always there for him, even when he ran for fun. Once, Santee challenged his fraternity brothers to a race after they razzed him for all the press attention he was getting. He would run the thirteen and a half miles from Tonganoxie to Lawrence against twenty-seven of them, each one taking a half mile. What started out as a fraternity stunt quickly captured the imagination of the town, and on a frigid December morning, with highway patrol cars and fans lining the highway, they began.

Santee quickly went into the lead over freshman football player Ralph Moody. Wearing a heavy blue sweatsuit and using woolen gym socks over his hands to protect from the cold, he finished his first mile in 4:41. Then he eased into a 5:36 average mile pace and continued on pace to whip his fraternity brothers by over 400 yards. Throughout the race, Easton, positioned in the back of a station wagon, called out Santee's mile times and heckled the other runners.

Stunts aside, Easton told Santee—and the press—that he was on course to become the best miler in the United States, and perhaps the world. He just needed more time to develop. Santee knew, however, that when it came to the four-minute mile, time wasn't on his side. Landy had put the barrier under threat, and with European milers like Englishman Roger Bannister and Belgian Gaston Reiff starting their seasons soon, it might be broken within months. Santee wanted his chance.

He enjoyed the attention he received just commenting about the possibility. "I don't know when it will be," he told a journalist, "but I'll run it, you can be sure of that. I'm as certain I can run the four-minute mile as you are that you can drive your car home." Santee basked in the media's limelight, and brash comments like this only heightened its intensity. He was also aware that if he were to achieve the goal, he would win more than just newspaper headlines. As an amateur college athlete, the only people getting rich from his efforts were the race promoters.

When the KU team returned from the Drake Relays, Easton summoned Santee to his office at Robinson Gymnasium. Santee headed over, as always walking quickly and with purpose in his cowboy boots. He climbed to the gym's third floor, taking the steps two at a time, ready to face Easton and answer for what had happened at the event. He hoped to convince his coach to let him concentrate on the mile.

Easton was waiting for him behind his old wooden schoolteacher's desk scattered with newspaper and magazine clippings. The small office was crowded with filing cabinets, trophies, and pictures of his athletes and teams through the years. As usual, he went straight to the point. "I didn't think you acted in a professional and appropriate way yesterday."

"Yes, sir," Santee said.

"You were insubordinate and rude."

"Those guys didn't hold up their end. I was mad."

"Well, I know that, Wes, but that's part of life. You can't always have what you want." Easton was calm, his voice even. "I didn't want to be a dropout from the race, even though you had to run like the dickens to get second. Do you understand my position?"

Santee nodded. Easton led him outside, where they sat down on the steps. It was one of those brilliant Kansas afternoons when the blue sky seemed to stretch to the ends of the earth. "I don't mind running for the team," Santee said. "But when do I get to run for myself?"

"Well, I've been thinking about how we mesh these things together."

The scene at the Drake Relays had demonstrated to Easton that Santee couldn't be held back any longer. "I want you to continue to run for the team," Easton said. "But when we get down to certain meets, you will enter the open mile event only."

These were the words Santee had been waiting for months

to hear. "You're the one to run the four-minute mile," Easton said confidently. "But you still need to improve. You're going to have to do different workouts than everybody else. You need to put more pressure on yourself."

Over the next two hours they talked about how Santee would ratchet up his training and about arranging for a "rabbit" to pace him through at least the first three-quarters of his record mile attempts. They also discussed Bannister, Landy, and others who they thought might have a chance at breaking the barrier. At last, it was clear to Santee that Easton wanted this as much as he did.

CHAPTER 9

JOHN LANDY WAS hard at work in his final year of agricultural science at the University of Melbourne. He was still deciding whether to go into farming or teaching as a career, but he knew he wanted to be able to travel and work outdoors. His father, who by the age of twenty-five had launched his own accountancy firm, advised him that it was unwise to pursue sport to the detriment of his career prospects. "There are more important things in life," he told his son, and Landy agreed. He planned to retire from athletics within eighteen months.

But that did not mean his focus wavered. If anything, it intensified because of the short time he had left. He had already achieved the two goals he set after leaving Helsinki: beating Don MacMillan's record and winning the Australian Championships. Now he wanted to break the world mile record and claim victory in the mile at the British Empire and Commonwealth Games in August 1954.

Success would guarantee him renown as the world's best miler, but it was not Landy's ambition to be famous or admired. Running drew out the best that was in him, as if he were plumbing the depths of his character. The downside of his success was that now every race he entered came with the expectation that he would break a record—and it was the four-minute mile that most people had in mind. Anything less was now considered not good enough. When he competed in the Australian Championships mile in Perth on Saturday, January 22, 1953, he finished seventy yards ahead of the closest runner in 4:04.2. The crowd greeted the announced time with silence, shrugs, and a disappointed early departure. It was the disheartening response that Landy was beginning to expect. Before the race, he had told a local reporter, "I'll do my best. If it comes, it comes, but, if it doesn't, for heck's sake, have the gate open. This crowd will lynch me."

As Landy's competitive season in the Southern Hemisphere came to an end and he started his training to prepare for the next one, spring had arrived in the Northern Hemisphere. Roger Bannister was visiting Oxford. He had fond memories of his time at Exeter College—its garret rooms, the dining hall lined with stained-glass windows and oil paintings, and the quadrangle where students lounged on the grass. His university days were over, but he still felt a strong attachment to the town—particularly to its track, where he hoped to make history.

He crossed Magdalen Bridge, the waters of the Isis flowing below, and headed toward Iffley Road. When he first arrived in Oxford, as a freshman student in 1946, he had found the track in shameful disrepair. At roughly 600 yards per lap (three laps to a mile), the oval was misshapen and suffered from poor drainage. In some places, old brick was exposed—a hazard for anyone in spikes. Bannister had raised the money to have it bulldozed and replaced with a new cinder track, 440 yards around and six lanes wide to meet international specifications. He wanted Iffley Road to be the site of his greatest success.

The annual AAA versus Oxford University meet on May 2 was the first chance of the 1953 season for athletes to make their mark after months of training. Given the smaller number of runners in the mile race, there would be none of the jostling and elbow work that characterized larger competitions. A fine setup for breaking a record.

Chris Chataway had agreed to pace Bannister through to the three-quarter-mile mark. He was better suited for three miles, and, since victory was not in the cards for him, he chose to help instead. The stocky redhead was two and a half years Bannister's junior, and he had always considered Bannister a distant and senior figure until they roomed together in Helsinki and became friends. There was nobody else in the field who had the ability to push Bannister through the entire race, particularly the critical last lap, and being paced through the first three laps was the only way Bannister had a chance at the four-minute barrier.

In the two months since Bannister began his intense track work, his fitness had improved dramatically, despite a rough period of irregular hours caused by midwife duties at St. Mary's. After an Easter break spent hiking in Wales, where he drank from mountain streams and dashed down steep screes as fast as his legs could carry him, he ran a three-quarter-mile trial in one second over three minutes. Two weeks later, on April 13, he ran an 880-yard trial in 1:52.1, showing how well tuned his speed was. He had reached his peak—and just at the right moment.

The AAA versus Oxford University match always drew a crowd, and the stands and surrounding banks of grass around the Iffley Road track were filled by three o'clock—fifteen minutes before the mile race was to start. Having consumed only a glass of orange juice mixed with glucose for lunch (his own special concoction), Bannister did his usual twenty-minute warm-up jog in his sweatsuit and readied himself for the race.

His focus on an all-out attempt was clear. Over the past week, he had gradually become more and more excited about this day. Soon he would channel this excitement, "to release," he later said, "every ounce of mental and physical energy I possessed over four minutes." The race was called, and the athletes, including Olympic steeplechasers Chris Brasher and John Disley and milers Derek Burfitt and John Bryant, lined up at the starting line to the left of the stands. They tensed as the starter raised the gun. *Bang!* They were off.

Chataway jumped into the lead within a few strides. It was an unusually fast early pace and left the rest of the field trying to keep up. Chataway finished the first lap in 62.1 seconds, with Bannister a few yards behind him. Chataway increased his pace, unsure of how fast he had run the first lap and getting no information from the timekeepers despite calling to them. Bannister remained second, sure in his rhythm. Disley moved into third place. The rest of the field was left behind.

Chataway crossed the half-mile mark in 2:04.1. It was too slow. Battling against a strong wind, he spent himself completely in the third lap, struggling to finish it in 60.9 seconds, for a three-quarter-mile time of 3:05. Only a few strides later he bowed out of the race, almost veering into the long-jump pit, dizzy from fatigue.

"Only the silky-striding Bannister was still in contention," Norris McWhirter wrote in his *Athletics World* account of the race. "Serene and now alone Bannister sailed on." Into the last lap, Bannister still had speed in reserve. His training had given him the endurance to follow Chataway at a harsh pace without exhausting his final kick. He delivered it now, pushing past the pain that was beginning to seize his legs.

At the 1,500-meter mark, Bannister registered 3:47, only 1.8 seconds slower than his time in the Olympic final against the best in the world. He sprinted for the remaining 120 yards, giving everything he had to complete the mile in 4:03.6. It was his best time by over four seconds, a new British record, and the fifth-fastest mile ever recorded.

"Roger Made It Look Easy" said the *News of the World* after the race. "Amazing Mile by Bannister" read another headline. Bannister's 4:03.6 may have put him back in the good graces of the press, but he cared little for what they thought. What he did now know for certain was that "the four-minute mile was not out of reach. It was only a question of time."

In mid-May 1953, Wes Santee and Bill Easton sat down in front of a television set to watch a replay of an interview with Finnish miler Denis Johansson. Reports had it that Johansson was shooting his mouth off about his upcoming race against Santee and Gaston Reiff at the Compton Invitational in June. "I think Santee will someday be a great miler," Johansson said, in grainy black and white. "But he still has to develop more physically and mentally. He's too unstable, flighty and cocky."

Santee could hardly believe his ears. Who was this guy? Johansson's best time in the mile was 4:08.3, and Santee had bettered that. Sure, the Finn had seen him fail miserably in the 5,000 meters in Helsinki, but that was nearly a year ago.

Johansson continued: "It may be some years yet before he really blossoms, and his mental attitude could do more to hold him back than his physical development, which hasn't far to go. I think that Santee is good enough to set a fast pace, but lack of experience in big-time competition is against him."

Santee boiled over. "I'll get you," he shouted, shaking his fist at the television. Easton tried to calm him down, but he didn't try very hard. He wanted Santee fired up for the race, and Johansson was stoking the flames nicely.

The Compton Invitational was Santee's best chance at the four-minute mile that season. The clay track was fast, the weather typically good, and the field was the best he would see all year. This competition was important since Easton's attempt to get someone to be a pacesetter for Santee had hit a brick wall with the AAU, the organization that had prevented him from representing the United States in the 1,500 meters at Helsinki.

The AAU was founded in 1888 by a group of private athletic clubs led by the New York Athletic Club. Its mission was to promote amateur sports and codify its rules. By 1912, the AAU ruled US track and field, most significantly by controlling eligibility for the Olympics. Since then, the organization had tended to its power carefully. They made it clear to Bill Easton that if pacesetting was even suspected to have occurred at Compton, or at any other meet for that matter, Santee's time would be disqualified.

Competition from the likes of Denis Johansson, particularly after his remarks about Santee's maturity, was the next best thing to a pacesetter. It was important that Santee have a go at the four-minute mile, and soon. Bannister had recently posted a 4:03.6 mile, and Landy was already training hard for his next season. Compton was Santee's best shot.

On Sunday, May 24, Santee gave Johansson a preview of what he could expect in California. At the Big Seven Conference Championships in Ames, Iowa, Santee blazed the mile in 4:06.3, taking the national collegiate mile record from Glenn Cunningham, who had held it for eighteen years. After the run, Santee said, "I caught my quarters right on time and the race went exactly as Uncle Bill and I had planned." Forty minutes later, he won the half mile in 1:50.8, and his team romped home to an overall victory.

When Easton and Santee arrived in Los Angeles on

Thursday, June 4, the event's promoter, Al Franken, picked them up in his Ford convertible. Franken had a knack for making people feel like they were the most important person in the world, and he escorted Santee around town for a series of television and radio appearances. There was even a brief encounter with Marilyn Monroe. Santee was completely dazzled by the glamour of it all.

Franken arranged for the press to watch Santee training, which fueled even more excitement about the next day's race. Santee was a promoter's dream. He was relaxed with the reporters, to whom he declared his confidence about winning—and, yes, breaking the four-minute-mile barrier was a distinct possibility as well.

On Friday morning, Santee went for a walk after his prerace breakfast of oatmeal and hot tea and honey. Back at the hotel, Bill Easton read the morning papers. "Santee Set to Teach Finnish Runner Lesson," predicted one of the headlines. The *Los Angeles Herald and Express* printed a cartoon showing Santee racing around a clock, with Reiff and Johansson not far behind. The caption read, "The Kansas Cyclone, Wes Santee, prodded by Reiff and Johansson, could well be the boy to break through the 4 minute barrier!" Franken had obviously done his job in drumming up attention. Now it was time to put all the hype aside and prepare for the race.

The mile was scheduled for 9:10. Four hours beforehand, Santee had some toast and more hot tea and honey. This was his ritual, and he never deviated from it. With one hour to go, he put on his sweatsuit top and went outside the stadium to do some light running and stretching. Then he returned to the infield, where he ran some sprints, working up a sweat. After that, he returned to the locker room, changed into a clean singlet and shorts, and lay down on the training table for fifteen minutes, hands on his stomach, eyes closed.

He spoke to nobody, not even to Easton. They had already worked everything out between them. Just moments before the gun was set to go off, Santee stepped to the starting line, oblivious to the noise around him, his one thought that of crushing Johansson.

Gaston Reiff went into an early lead and finished the lap in first position, followed within a few yards by Santee, then Johansson, Bob McMillen, and Russ Bonham. When Santee heard the lap time—62.7 seconds—he knew it was slow, but his moment to strike had to wait. Reiff continued to set the pace for the field through the second lap, registering a half-mile time of 2:05.2. The crowd sighed, resigned to a slow race. Franken yanked on his hair; he hadn't brought all these mile stars together to run a mediocre race.

Santee was equally anxious: The first half mile was too

slow for a record time. He had to do something soon. In the third lap, Johansson sped quickly past Reiff, and Santee followed. The crowd continued to groan and boo. In the back straight of the third lap, Santee lost his patience. He charged, nearly into a sprint, and swept past Johansson before the end of the straight. The Finn couldn't believe it. What was this kid doing going into a sprint 700 yards from the finish? He had made his move too early.

Santee didn't think so. He had to go for broke if he was to have a shot at the four-minute barrier. The crowd loved him for his boldness. Johansson increased his tempo, knowing that if Santee put too much distance between them, the race was over. By the end of the third lap, the Finn had won back a yard from Santee, with Reiff six yards back from the lead. Santee had run an incredible 58.2 third lap, and the scoreboard read an elapsed time of 3:03.5. Cheers erupted from the stands. This might be a fast race after all.

Santee continued driving furiously, to the bewilderment of Johansson. Santee's final 440 yards was run in a heart-stopping 55 seconds. But he was tiring and struggled to maintain pace. He leaned forward into the tape, breasting it twelve yards ahead of Johansson in 4:02.4: the fastest mile ever run by an American. The crowd chanted his name as he slowed into a walk.

Johansson came up to him. "You guys are crazy," he said,

barely able to talk. "I never had anyone sprint 700 yards before the finish." Santee smiled and shook his hand, as he often did with his competitors after a race. He could always tell how tired they were by the strength of their handshake. Johansson was exhausted.

News of the race made headlines from Los Angeles to New York to London to Melbourne. Johansson was the first to say how great Santee was, followed by something of an apology: "He taught me not to pop off so much." Reiff predicted that if Santee were to go head-to-head with Bannister, Santee would win. Most reports, however, talked of the four-minute mile: "Santee Admits Getting Closer to Phantom Four-Minute Mile" and "Jet-Propelled Santee Flirts with 4:00 Mile." If some people had yet to hear that Santee was out to break the barrier, they most certainly knew now.

CHAPTER 10

AMONG MELBOURNE'S SMALL community of athletes, the latest news was traded like good gossip. The few among them who subscribed to magazines like *Track & Field News* and the *Athletic Review* were highly valued purveyors of information. Les Perry shared his magazines with his friends, including John Landy. It was understood that they would then be passed along to others. Somehow the dogeared copies eventually found their way back.

The recent write-ups told of how Bannister and Santee were nearing Hägg's record and setting their sights on the four-minute mile. The Englishman's and American's summer was Landy's winter, and even though he received invitations to compete in the USA and England, he was still in the middle of his studies. This was a great disappointment to track promoters, who were always conspiring to bring the three together.

The only time Landy saw the other two run was when a segment of a race was included in the newsreels shown at the cinema. These were always a couple of months behind. But even though he was eager to see or hear news about

Bannister's and Santee's runs, Landy felt that he had his own course to follow, and he wouldn't let himself be rushed by anyone. The pursuit of the mile record was not about being the first to cross the four-minute threshold. It was about proving how good he was. He was running for himself, not for national honor.

When his 1953 season finished, Landy made it clear that he intended to keep training throughout the winter. "It won't be any good my dropping training until next spring, if I want to run fast miles [next] December and after," he said to reporter Joseph Galli. He was convinced that a more intense regime would produce better times than before, regardless of the slow tracks and lack of competition in Australia.

In late June 1953, frost from the Australian winter on the ground, he stuck to his approach, going for long runs on the coast road, nearly in a trance from the rhythm of his feet striking the ground. Landy never saw his running as a sacrifice. He liked the discipline it required and liked feeling his body growing to tolerate ever-increasing levels of stress. He knew that come his first race in December, when the nervous energy had expired after the first lap, he would need the conditioning from these training runs to sustain his speed to the very end.

Australian miler Don MacMillan was studying quietly in his student hostel in London when someone down the hall shouted, "Hey, Don, you're wanted on the phone." It was unusual for him to get a call, so he hurried downstairs. Curious, he picked up the receiver.

"Roger here. Roger Bannister."

"G'day, Roger." MacMillan couldn't understand why Bannister had phoned him. They hadn't spoken in a while.

"How are you running?"

"Not too good at the moment. I have a sore leg. How are you?"

"I'm going very well. What do you think about Wes Santee?" News of the American's proximity to the mile barrier would have been hard to miss. The British papers had covered the Compton Invitational win as well as Santee's announcement that he would make another attempt on June 27, the following Saturday.

"Do you think he could do it?" MacMillan asked.

"I think he might be able to, but I want to beat him to it." There was a pause. "Would you be prepared to help me?"

"I'll do what I can, but I'm not very fit."

Bannister explained. Norris McWhirter had convinced the director of a schoolboys' meet (the Surrey Schools AAA

Neal Bascomb

Championships at Motspur Park) to add a special invitation mile in their schedule. With the six-hour time difference between Britain and the United States, Bannister might be able to pip Santee to the post. He needed two pacesetters to help him make the attempt. "I'd like you to run as far as you can at 60 seconds a lap. Chris Brasher will take me around the last lap."

"All right, I'll do my best," MacMillan said. If he could not push Landy to a four-minute mile, it was better to have Bannister, a fellow British Empire man, run it than an American, he thought.

The clandestine nature and overt pacing of the race were not ideal. But McWhirter persuaded Bannister that he had to try. "Santee's going to do it. And you simply wouldn't want to let him do it."

Since the 4:03.6 mile that highlighted Bannister's potential as the first four-minute miler, the pressure to break the barrier had only intensified. The press hounded him at every turn, asking whether this day would be the day. On May 23, he had run a slow race at White City Stadium, and a group of fans booed and harassed him for not breaking the barrier, even though he easily beat the rest of the field. The next day, the newspapers accused him of "disappointing a big crowd" and "scarcely fulfilling the expectations of the 20,000 people present."

96

When he then ran a record-breaking 1:51.9 half mile on May 30, through a blustery wind, he barely warranted mention in the papers. The British public wanted another big achievement to match the recent conquest of Everest by Edmund Hillary and the coronation of Queen Elizabeth II. Anything less wasn't going to be good enough.

On the morning of June 27, McWhirter drove Bannister, MacMillan, and Brasher from London to Motspur Park. Brasher was not a particularly fast mile runner, but he wouldn't have to be, given their pacesetting arrangements. Two official timekeepers were on hand to validate the time. McWhirter himself would serve as the third timekeeper. AAA officials Jack Crump and Harold Abrahams were also present, but there were few others, apart from the 1,000 schoolboys who were there for their event.

The three runners warmed up on the adjacent cricket field while the groundsmen rolled and then lightly watered the cinders in preparation for the race. At 1:50 p.m., under a clear sky and with only a slight breeze blowing into the finishing straight, the three runners lined up.

As planned, MacMillan led from the beginning, Bannister tethered closely behind. Brasher moved purposefully slow since his work wouldn't start until the end of the third lap. The Australian proved a superbly even pacesetter for the first two laps. In the third lap, Bannister yelled, "Wide open, Don"—meaning go at full throttle—but MacMillan stalled. He was exhausted. Bannister hesitated, losing a precious second, before shifting past the Australian to finish the third lap in 3:01.8.

From the track side, Norris McWhirter called out the time. The schoolboys munched their sandwiches, not sure why these men were running in the middle of their meet. At the ringing of the bell, Brasher, having run only two laps, was in position to bring Bannister around the last 440 yards. He yelled a stream of expletives over his shoulder for his friend to hurry up.

Bannister crossed the 1,500-meter mark in 3:44.8—a time that would have earned him gold in Helsinki. In the last 120 yards he started to "climb the ladder." Exhaustion took over, his head tilted up, his knees lifted, and his arms swung higher and higher to get every inch out of the stride. Brasher shouted back, "Come on, Roger!" Bannister fought mightily to the tape, but it was not fast enough. He clocked a 4:02.

The schoolboys erupted in cheers, more from believing that Bannister had caught Brasher in the last straight to win than from realizing that they had just witnessed the third-fastest mile in history.

Although Bannister had clocked an incredible time, the mood was somber afterward. It had taken a lot to arrange this event, and it had been for nothing. Norris McWhirter telephoned later to say that Santee had also failed in his bid, running 4:07.6 in Dayton. Bannister knew he wouldn't be able to summon the energy to make another attempt against the clock that summer. He desperately hoped that Santee would not either.

There was a groundswell of reaction to Bannister's 4:02. Some called the race "fixed" and "unsporting." Jesse Abramson in the *New York Herald Tribune* wrote, "The world obviously would like to see a 4:00 mile, but let's keep it kosher in a regularly fixed race." Many in the British press felt the same: The *Daily Mail* declared the race not "bona fide," and the *Daily Mirror* called Bannister a "clock-runner" who was "brilliant at running against that rhythmically moving second hand on the clock face, but has little relish for the cut-and-thrust of flying spikes and jolting elbows." British amateur officials were considering whether or not the record time should be ratified.

"Maybe I could run a four-minute mile behind one of my father's ranch horses," Santee replied when journalists asked him what he thought of Bannister's Motspur Park paced race. "If that's what you want."

Santee was in Europe for a summer tour sponsored by the AAU. His trip was supposed to provide him with the opportunity to break the four-minute barrier on the fast tracks and against the top-class competition that Europe provided. One month in, and he had experienced very little rest, a lot of travel, bad food, meager prizes, and a grinding schedule of races. In total, the two-month tour schedule had him running in twenty-two races. The entire time he was away, he was either at the track or in transit. He missed Coach Easton, and he particularly missed Danna. He wrote to her almost every day.

In Berlin, Santee had had enough. For weeks he and his American teammates had packed stadiums with tens of thousands of fans. Meanwhile, amateur officials in each country they traveled to (who worked closely with the track promoters selling tickets) were providing them with spartan meals. If they wanted dessert or a second cup of coffee, they had to pay. If one of them didn't perform to the required standard, reprimands were handed out. And if Santee came in first in a race—a common occurrence—all he got as a prize was a plaque, a mechanical pencil, or an inexpensive watch.

What he should have been doing was conserving his strength for one or two good races, like the British Games in a few days' time. Instead, he was working day in and day out for little to no reward. Having labored many long hours for his father on the ranch without pay, Santee knew when someone was taking advantage of him.

He asked a German official if he could pool several of his prizes and swap them for an Agfa camera. At the time, this was the Rolls-Royce of cameras, and Bill Easton had suggested that Santee should try to get his hands on one when he was in Europe. The official told Santee that he would take care of it, but when Santee followed up, he was told that the camera was more expensive than the amateur rules allowed and that "they could not consider any such demands."

That set Santee off. After all the money they had made on him—and the sacrifice involved on his part—they could at least provide him with a camera. The official said that there was nothing he could do, but, regardless, "We want you to stay on and run another race."

"To hell with you. I'm not staying here."

Santee stormed out of the room, slamming the door behind him. Little was said of the affair, but everyone knew that Santee would have to pay for his outburst one way or another. Amateur officials did not suffer this kind of behavior from their athletes.

After Germany, Santee went to Finland, and from there to London for the British Games. He hoped to compete against Roger Bannister, but on his arrival he learned that Bannister was busy with his medical exams and had backed out. Still, the mile race was a big international affair: Gunder Hägg, Sydney Wooderson, and Paavo Nurmi were all taking part, and with Denis Johansson and several of Britain's best middle-distance men also in the event, including Chris Chataway, Bill Nankeville, and Gordon Pirie, this was a prime chance for Santee to get the competition he needed for a record attempt.

But he was simply exhausted from the traveling and the constant competition. By the fourth lap, when most expected him to explode to the finish line, he had nothing left to give. Pirie sprinted past him in the back straight to win by three yards in 4:06.8. "I've run seven races—one every other day," Santee told reporters afterward. "I'm more than a bit tired."

When he returned to the USA, pundits declared that Santee risked burning out before he reached his prime if he continued to compete so often. Santee discounted the claims, but privately he knew he wasn't being given the support he needed to break the mile barrier. He wanted to be able to enlist pacesetters, to go to events featuring top-class competition, and to have enough breathing room beforehand to prepare and focus properly. His confrontation with amateur officials in Berlin had ignited a firestorm, so his chances of ever receiving this support were almost nonexistent. Nonetheless, he still felt that the four-minute mile was his to run first.

In September 1953, Bannister felt like he was fighting an uphill battle. He had started his final year at St. Mary's and was set to take his General Medical Council exams the following summer. His plan was to hang up his running spikes in August 1954 after the British Empire and Commonwealth Games in Vancouver and the European Athletic Championships in Bern, and he wanted to finish his running career on a high by winning these two championships and by breaking the mile barrier.

For the first time, however, he wasn't sure he could do it alone. The previous season had ended badly. He suffered a thrashing in the press for the Motspur Park attempt, and this was followed by the embarrassment of the British Amateur Athletic Board's decision to reject his 4:02 mile as a British record. The board did not consider the event a bona fide competition according to the rules. Bannister accepted this decision without appeal. In hindsight, he knew it was wrong to have attempted the record in conditions so far outside those of a normal race, but at the time, there seemed to be no other choice if he was to be the first to break the record.

For seven years, Bannister had followed his own training

methods, methodically improving his times all the way. But even though the list of his championship wins and record times was pages long, he still found himself coming up short in reaching his greatest athletic ambitions. So it was that he took his first step away from his "lone wolf" approach and started training with a partner, Chris Brasher, who also ran each lunchtime at the Paddington track.

For the past year Brasher had been training with an Austrian coach, Franz Stampfl. The sessions took place in the Duke of York's Barracks in Chelsea on Friday evenings and in Battersea Park on the weekend. Stampfl had given Brasher a training schedule, part of which he fulfilled by running with Bannister at the Paddington track. On occasion they were joined by Chris Chataway, who had lately started training with the Austrian coach as well.

After a few weeks, Brasher and Chataway convinced Bannister to come and meet Stampfl. Brasher was insistent. "It is absolutely necessary to have someone to whom you can turn, who is entirely honest with you," he said. "Someone you know will not give spurious advice."

Bannister's failure to break the mile record the previous season had convinced him that he had gone as far as he could on his own. In October, after a day at the hospital, he went with Chataway and Brasher to the Duke of York's Barracks to meet Stampfl and listen to what he had to say.

The training ground was adjacent to a barracks that housed Territorial Army soldiers, the British Army's volunteer reserve force. In the early evenings the track and a drill hall were available, and Stampfl had arranged with the army to use the facilities to coach athletes. He charged one shilling per session.

When Bannister first entered the large hall, Stampfl was leading a group of forty athletes through warm-up exercises, mostly push-ups and calisthenics. His strongly accented voice boomed throughout the drill hall. Stampfl was barrel-chested and almost six feet tall. When he approached Bannister and his companions, he looked even bigger, his stride strong, features sharp, and eyes alight. Despite being in a room full of athletes in sports gear, he wore a Savile Row blazer, corduroy pants, and polished shoes.

Stampfl was a talented skier and javelin thrower, and had participated in the 1932 Olympics in Los Angeles in the javelin. Born in Vienna, Austria, in 1913, he moved to England in 1936 to attend Cambridge University. When Britain declared war on Germany, he tried to join the RAF but instead was interned as an "enemy alien." He went on a hunger strike to protest his imprisonment. In July 1940, he was en route to Canada with a host of other prisoners of war on the *Arandora Star* when a German U-boat torpedoed their ship in the North Atlantic. Stampfl survived in the sea for eight hours, struggling to stay afloat, before a rescue boat sighted him. Hundreds died, and those who survived were interned and then transported to Australia.

At the internment camp in Hay, New South Wales, Stampfl organized athletics, boxing, wrestling, and football matches to ease the desperation plaguing the POWs. He said that his motivation came from "an inner desire to survive and remain sane for myself and my friends in camp." When the war ended, he and his Australian wife moved to London. Although he had suffered terribly, he still admired the English, particularly their love for amateur sport, and he believed that their athletes could use his help.

By the fall of 1953, Stampfl was training athletes in everything from field events (javelin, hammer throw, and discus) to distance running. He knew a great deal about interval methods and racing techniques, but his most valuable insights came from an understanding of what it took to get the best out of an athlete.

Franz Stampfl was unlike anyone Bannister had ever met, and he sensed immediately that this coach truly knew about courage and determination. He agreed to come back the following Friday.

CHAPTER 11

ONE SEPTEMBER NIGHT, at two in the morning, John Landy was running alone along Melbourne's Dandenong Road. The streetlights cast an eerie orange glow through the fog, and Landy was ascending a straight uphill stretch when he saw a car's headlights coming toward him, swerving left and right. The driver was obviously drunk. Landy slowed a little and waited for the car to pass. It stopped a few feet ahead of him.

Although Landy made a habit of running along that particular road, he understood that most people would be suspicious of someone doing so in the middle of the night. The driver rolled down the window, and Landy stepped up to the side of the car. "Who do you think you are, mate?" the inebriated driver asked. "Bloody Landy?"

Rather than admit he was, indeed, bloody Landy, he headed off down the road. Not every Australian could recognize him, but they had all most certainly heard of him.

From July 21 to September 30, Landy averaged ten 600-yard fast runs daily, at roughly a 66-second quarter-mile pace. In between each run, he jogged 600 yards. Since he was studying for his final exams in October and November, he decided to train at double his normal rate on alternate days. On the off days, he jogged at a five- to six-minute-a-mile pace for half an hour. On the hard days in October, he ran twenty 600-yard fast laps with a jog in between each (approximately 14 miles a night), and in November he ran twenty 440-yard laps at a 62-second pace. Night after night he pushed himself a little bit harder.

His first race was on November 21. In his mind, this was just an early season tune-up run, and he had to repeatedly deny claims that he was gunning for the "magic mile." Regardless, he ran a 4:09.2, over seven seconds faster than his first race the previous year. After he finished his last exam and had run two more tune-up races at Olympic Park, he declared himself ready for his season's first fast run. He was in self-described "top condition."

It was one year to the day since he surprised the world with his first spectacular mile, and there was a world of difference at Olympic Park compared to the previous year. For a start, the prime minister of Australia was in attendance, and all that week the papers had drum-rolled the event. The immense pressure was palpable, but Landy knew that if he felt too tense, he wouldn't run well. He had trained for this day and was confident that he had the speed—as long as he didn't force it.

From the start, Landy raced into the lead, and it was clear within 200 yards that he was out for the record. John Marks tried to push him through the first half mile, hanging as near as he could to the "Meteor Miler" as he clocked 58.2 seconds in the first lap and 60.4 in the second lap. At that point, Marks dropped out of the race, unable to continue. Les Perry struggled behind Landy through the next lap, doing what he could to force competition on his friend. But it was no use. Landy might as well have been in the race alone. In his mind, he was. The clock was his only competition. Perry stumbled off the track at the three-quarter mark.

The bell rang at 3:00.2. Having heard the time, Landy thought he could at least beat Hägg's world record of 4:01.4. It was in the last lap that his hard training would bear fruit. The crowd was on its feet, clapping loudly. He continued to run well, maintaining his pace through the back straight and into the last turn. But when he came into the straight, he suddenly felt like the finish line was miles away.

A cruel gust of wind seemed to stop him flat, even though his legs kept moving. The wind ruined the rhythm of his stride, making it uneven. Within five yards of the tape, he slowed noticeably. His time was 4:02, only one-tenth of a second faster than his best mile the previous year, in spite of all the training.

Landy shook hands with the prime minister, smiled for a few photographs, and retreated to the locker room, where he was physically sick. Then he came back out to speak with the reporters. His frustration was clear: "No one outside of sport can imagine the grind of years of continuous training . . . Frankly, I think the four-minute mile is beyond my capabilities. Two seconds may not sound much, but to me it's like trying to break through a brick wall."

No doubt some of this statement was intended to reduce the pressure he felt was being put on him. Privately he thought he still could lower his time. He had only just finished his exams, and with some more race preparation, he was sure he could run faster.

The next day, he left for Tallarook, an area of bush sixty miles northeast of Melbourne, to forget about running for a while. He and several others devoted to butterfly collecting were interested in finding a stenciled hairstreak (*Jalmenus ictinus*), a butterfly that had not been captured in Victoria in more than half a century. Landy savored these trips, net in hand, looking out for a particular wing pattern and color. It was a fulfilling pursuit, one that running had taken him away from. He did manage to find a stenciled hairstreak, with its dark brown wings that had a patch of metallic blue in the middle. It was a triumph that gave him, as he later said, "equal pleasure as running 4:02 for the mile."

At the University of Kansas, a blanket of snow lay over the ground and hung heavy on the trees. Most students had not yet returned from the winter break, and only a few footprints speckled the snow-covered paths. Underneath the concrete stands at the stadium, in a corridor only a few feet wide, cold and dank with condensation, Wes Santee was running.

Each time he passed Bill Easton and disappeared around the corner, Easton sounded his foghorn. Its blast reverberated against the low ceiling. Santee ran unconcerned, feeling strong as he took each stride. One lap to go in his three-quarter-mile trial. He sensed the time was good. Usually he could judge his own pace over a quarter mile within a second of the stopwatch. After crossing the finish line, he slowed and turned back to Easton, who held out his stopwatch. "Look at this! You're ready. You're ready," Easton said. "If you can run 2:58 in this rat hole, you could have walked it on a real track."

Santee knew he was right. It was early January 1954, two weeks before his four-minute mile attempt, which was to be held during the halftime break in the Pro Bowl, at the Los Angeles Coliseum. He was indeed ready, and Al Franken, who had organized the race, was expecting great things.

Easton had ratcheted up his training yet again. The goal

was for Santee to get used to running a 4:04 to 4:06 mile so that doing so was more a matter of habit than strenuous effort. Given the right factors—namely, good competition and fine track conditions—and Santee would have a shot at the barrier.

The payoff from all the training was obvious. In November, Santee had led his Jayhawks team to victory, placing first in the Big Seven and NCAA cross-country championships. On the last day of 1953, at the Sugar Bowl in New Orleans, he dashed to a 4:04.2 mile, which was amazing not only because the track was soggy from rain but also because he ran the final lap in a stupefying 55 seconds. After the race, an Associated Press reporter hit the wires with the following question: "Wes Santee . . . John Landy . . . Roger Bannister . . . Who is going to be the first to reach the end of the rainbow and run the fabled four-minute mile?"

According to the press, the only person able to catch Wes Santee was Danna Denning, his newly announced fiancée. A picture of them wearing matching cowboy shirts was plastered across papers under the headline "The Girl That Finally Caught Wes." Danna gave him all the more incentive to do well.

Early on January 17, the day of the Pro Bowl, Santee left the Ambassador Hotel in Los Angeles to take his morning walk. But when he stepped out on the grass, his foot sank into six inches of water. It had rained through the night. A few hours later, Franken came by to take him to the stadium. He was shaking his head, obviously distraught. "I'm really sorry, Wes. It hasn't rained like this in five years. The track is flooded." As they drove to the Coliseum, the sun finally appeared in the sky, but it was too late. The track was standing under water, and the race had to be canceled.

Santee was devastated. He was in perfect form *now*. Landy was at the height of his season, and Bannister was sure to run well as soon as he started. His own outdoor season wouldn't begin for several months, and an ongoing dispute with the AAU, over the camera incident in Germany among other things, meant that his prospects for competing in any top-flight races were in serious jeopardy.

Santee and the AAU were heading toward a collision. He was seen as a threat to the organization's power. Because he sold out the meets in which he participated, particularly with his penchant for publicity and the mile barrier ever on the horizon, he had a degree of power himself. Then the *Saturday Evening Post* published a profile by Bob Hurt titled "Sure I'll Run the Four-Minute Mile," which quoted Santee as saying, "I'd like to run for about ten more years. But I'm not going to run unless I can make it pay. I wouldn't want to waste ten years." Hurt also wrote that Santee was hoping to earn enough "expenses" from his track meets to buy a farm.

The AAU went ballistic. No amateur under their watch would boast of such a thing. Santee denied saying these things, but the AAU appeared bent on bringing him down.

Thursday, January 21, 1954, was a clear, windless summer day in Melbourne. Crowds of people began to gather at Olympic Park for the special twilight meet featuring Landy. This was to be the race. Landy was on the front or back page of every Melbourne newspaper: "A Perfect Night for John's Mile" headlined the *Sun News-Pictorial*. "Flat-Out Attempt on 4.0 Mile," said the Melbourne *Age*. Dick Crossley, the venerated groundsman at Olympic Park, had personally rolled the track and declared it was in perfect condition.

As for Landy himself, he felt good to go. Finished with his studies, he was now able to train during the day in Central Park, and he had been doing a lot of speed work. Since his 4:02 mile six weeks before, he had run in two mile races, and in neither did he make a record attempt. Three days before the race, Landy took a much-needed break from his training and headed to the bush again, where he hunted for some butterflies to add to his collection. The night before the race, he slept for twelve hours. The only interruptions were calls from reporters and a batch of telegrams delivered to his door, wishing him good luck.

Landy's friend, half-miler Len McRae, picked him up at his house in his red Singer Six convertible, and drove him and quarter-miler Ian Ormsby to the stadium. Because of the traffic, they had to park on a nearby hill. Tickets could not be sold fast enough, and lines had formed hundreds of yards long behind the booths. The crowd was getting rowdy, anxious to get inside. Landy was astonished at the number of people in attendance—10,000, maybe 20,000. Typically, track events attracted 300 or 400 at most.

The athletes forced their way through the crowd, but it looked like it was going to be impossible to get to the front. They worried that they might miss their races. "How are we going to get in?" McRae asked. The athletes decided that they would scale the eight-foot-high wire fence surrounding Olympic Park. They tossed their gym bags over, then climbed the pickets, making sure not to get stuck on the sharp points.

As they cleared the top, a highly regarded South Yarra doctor waiting with his son at the back of the line shouted, "Look at those louts, getting over the fence and not paying."

"Dad," the boy said, "that is John Landy."

By the time Landy had changed and begun his warm-up,

the crowd had swelled to such a size that they knocked down the fence and rushed inside the stadium. Some climbed on top of the tin roof over the grandstand. A wall of people had encircled the track, and many were standing on the outside lane. The place was total chaos.

When Landy took to the track, a few minutes before the race at 7:30 p.m., the fans cheered wildly. Newsreel cameras whirred, and cameras flashed, momentarily blinding the runners. The pressure was intense. Landy felt obligated to deliver a record or risk letting everybody down. He shook the hands of his competitors, then settled down in a crouch in the third lane from the inside, waiting for the gun. The crowd grew silent as 20,000 pairs of eyes were trained on Landy, willing him to break the barrier for the glory of Australia.

As usual, Landy went into the lead by the first turn and never looked back. Nobody could keep up with him. He had refused pacing, telling the other runners that if he suspected they weren't running to win, he would step off the track. If he broke the mile record, he wanted to have done it on his own.

He ran the first lap in 59 seconds and the second in 61.3. He couldn't hear his times being called, but he had a good sense of his own pace. All he could do was run at 100 percent effort and hope that it was enough. If the other factors aligned, he might break the record. When the bell clanged, the timekeepers read 3:02.1. The crowd was on its feet, their applause deafening.

Landy responded, looking to push faster, harder. But 200 yards from the finish, he felt as if someone had pulled the "master power switch," draining the energy from his legs. He fought the fatigue and the temptation to slow down and stretched to the finish, hoping it was enough. As he broke through the tape, the spectators threw programs, handkerchiefs, and hats into the air and gave him a standing ovation.

Landy waited for his time, uncertain whether he had broken the record or turned in another 4:02 performance. Finally the official time was announced on the loudspeakers: 4:02.4. Roiled with disappointment but unwilling to show it, Landy jogged forward, waving at the crowd, who continued to clap. "I thought I had it," he told the *Sun*'s Jack Dunn.

When he returned to Malvern East, his mother had organized a party for him. Although he had not broken the mile record, none of his friends or family bemoaned the fact. After all, he had won the race.

The next day, his run was characterized on the front pages as a "Magnificent Failure!" Denis Johansson, who was in Australia preparing for a race against Landy the following month, had a different viewpoint: "Landy is magnificent—the greatest mile runner I have seen. On a first-class cinder track with solid opposition he'll run 3:55 for the mile." Johansson promised to help him see it happen, raising the possibility of Landy traveling to Scandinavia at the end of the Australian season.

CHAPTER 12

ON FEBRUARY 10, Coach Easton and Wes Santee made one last effort to stop the AAU punishing Santee by revoking his amateur status. They vehemently denied reports from Germany that Santee had thrown a chair at the official who refused to give him the camera. They also made it clear that Bob Hurt from the *Saturday Evening Post* had misquoted Santee about trying to make money from his running. Even so, the AAU banned Santee from competing internationally for one year.

Soon after, Santee told reporters that he didn't need any competition to push him to run the mile record. He could do it anywhere, track and weather permitting, as long as his legs felt all right. But privately he later admitted, "I could do it up to a point, but there was something about competition that raised the bar. It's like someone pulls you along." While this ban was in place, good competition was going to be hard to find.

Bannister finished his last round of the day in the hospital, hung up his white coat, grabbed his gym bag, and left St.

Mary's, heading in the direction of Sloane Square. He was meeting Chris Chataway and Chris Brasher at the Duke of York's Barracks, as was now their Friday night routine. The weather was typical for February and no better than it had been during the past two weeks. A bitter wind threatened heavy showers and the occasional bit of hail, and a hard frost was forecast for that night.

Every week throughout the winter, the three had trained together. They measured their progress, strengthened their sense of working as a team, and soaked up Franz Stampfl's enthusiasm. The session started with calisthenics in the drill hall, alongside scores of other athletes, such as shot-putters and discus and javelin throwers. Stampfl ran them through a series of push-ups, stretching, and resistance exercises, not only increasing their upper-body strength but also fostering the sense of being part of a much larger group. After twenty minutes they took a brief rest and then hit the track.

Stampfl kept a watchful eye on the three runners as they went through their interval training together, yelling out to them from time to time: "Do it again!" "Harder!" "Faster! It's only pain!" Stampfl knew that Bannister was uncomfortable taking direction from a coach, so instead of imposing a regimen, he just offered suggestions and guidance, and he tried never to push too hard.

In Stampfl's opinion, Bannister needed three things to

run the four-minute mile: pacesetters to carry him through the first three laps, more strength in his legs, and complete belief in himself. Over the past three months he had worked hard to help Bannister realize these goals, not only because he had a passion for helping an athlete who was impassioned himself but also because if Bannister broke the barrier under his guidance, more athletes would come to him for coaching.

Two pacesetters would be needed, as the Motspur Park race had shown: one to take Bannister through the first half mile, and the second to bring him to the three-quarter mark. They had to be able to maintain evenly paced 60-second laps, and they had to be able to finish the race, to comply with amateur rules. Chataway and Brasher had both signed up to be the pacesetters. The training sessions were also good training for their own events: the steeplechase (Brasher) and the three-mile (Chataway). Plus, they wanted to be part of what would be a historic feat.

Physically, Bannister was very close to being capable of the achievement. At his level of fitness, improvement was difficult to discern, but running with Chataway and Brasher relieved the monotony, and Stampfl encouraged him week after week to keep at it. The systematic gradual increases of speed over several months had adapted his body to the stress.

Stampfl's greatest contribution to Bannister's attempt

to make history was his ability to inspire him. Although Bannister had the scientific understanding to refute the notion that the mile barrier couldn't be broken, believing he was the one to do it was another matter. "The great hurdle was the mental barrier," Stampfl said.

After their sessions at the Duke of York's track, Stampfl often joined the three men for dinner near Sloane Square. They would take refuge from the cold, enjoy a bottle of wine, and relax. Stampfl dominated their conversations, which usually started with a discussion of their training and how they were advancing, but as dinner progressed the conversation would shift to politics, art, philosophy. The Austrian coach read widely, and he could take every side of an argument, making for lively dinners that the three runners looked forward to after an exhausting session.

They also talked about Landy and Santee and how close they were coming to the four-minute mile. Week after week they nervously waited for the latest news from the USA and Australia.

The McWhirter twins continued to be their main source of information. Only three days before, they brought news that Landy had run another sub-4:03 mile, the fifth in his career. They knew about the kind of training sessions that Landy was running, and yet the Australian miler was coming up short again and again. Somehow he was stuck. But with reports confirming that Denis Johansson was bringing him to compete on Finland's fast tracks, anything was possible.

As for Santee, his threat was obvious. He had recently clocked a 4:02.6 mile on an indoor track. A meager forty-one minutes later he ran a 1:51.8 half mile. It was the "greatest double in American track history," exclaimed the latest issue of *Track and Field News*, and evidence that "the honor of running the first four-minute mile will be lodged in the USA." Santee was likely to better his time once the outdoor season began.

Their earliest opportunity to make a bid was at the AAA versus Oxford University meet in early May. Bannister understood that his goal would require not just ability and hard work but also luck, teamwork, and a dose of inspiration. Over the past sixteen months the mile barrier had withstood the greatest assaults ever made upon it. Bannister needed to throw every advantage he had at the "brick wall" to have a chance of breaking through it.

Two seconds had never seemed so long a time, but at least now he was part of a team, one that encouraged him when the training became tedious or when his confidence faltered. It was making all the difference.

Every spring, the University of Kansas hosted the Kansas Relays, welcoming athletes from around the country. It was a great excuse for a party, and on the morning of Saturday, April 17, preparations were in full gear. Fraternity and sorority members had been up since dawn finishing their floats for the grand parade. High school students, many of whom had never been out of their hometowns, ran about the campus, wearing varsity letter sweaters and feeling the excitement of college life. Cars jammed the streets, and hundreds lined the sidewalks for the parade. The sun shone brightly, and it looked like one of those glad-to-be-alive days that early spring does so well.

Santee didn't let the beehive of activity disturb his pre-race ritual. Today he was running in the Glenn Cunningham Mile, at 3:05 p.m. He had his breakfast of oatmeal and hot tea and honey and, a few hours later, walked down to the stadium to warm up. His calm exterior belied the fact that this was a big weekend, perhaps the biggest of his life. That day, he intended to claim the four-minute mile, and the following day he and Danna were getting married.

Three months had passed since his disappointment at the Pro Bowl. Since then, he had scorched up the track week after week, keeping fit while fueling the four-minute fever with every stunning performance. His team waltzed away with the Big Seven indoor championship, thanks in large part to him. At the first outdoor meet of the season in Austin, Texas, he earned the Jayhawks a world record in the sprint medley with an anchor half mile of 1:48.3, and he had led in the distance medley as well as the two-mile and four-mile relays.

A herd of reporters attended his every race, some from local papers but many from major national publications such as *Time*, *Newsweek*, the *Saturday Evening Post*, the *New York Times*, and the *New York Herald Tribune*. Santee liked their headlines: "Super Sonic Santee" and "Santee Is Star." The stories read even better: "Some night Santee's going to travel around that course like the wind and then he'll not only run the four-minute mile but he'll cut three or four seconds off that goal."

However, because of his team obligations, Santee was yet to have a good chance at the mile record. Easton had set those obligations aside for the Kansas Relays, to give Santee a shot. Together they had decided that the team was in a strong enough position to risk Santee competing in the open mile rather than in four team events, as he usually did.

With Landy heading to Finland and reports that Bannister was preparing for a paced attempt in early May, it was critical that they go for the four-minute mile straight away. Santee was also running out of time because his Marine officer training was scheduled for July, three months away. He was supposed to have done his twelve weeks of boot camp during his sophomore year, but he went to the Olympics instead.

After his junior year, the AAU arranged for another year's reprieve because it wanted him running in Europe. Further delay appeared impossible. It did not help that the AAU had banned Santee from competing internationally. With that restriction in place and the Marines demanding that he report for duty, the Compton Invitational was the best competition he would get. And the next best thing was the Kansas Relays.

By two o'clock on Saturday afternoon, the parade was done, and over 16,000 people had crowded into Memorial Stadium. It was hot and sultry, and the concessions stands quickly sold out of soda and ice. Spectators sheltered from the sun with umbrellas and fanned themselves with programs that featured a picture of "The Kansas Flyer—Wes Santee" on the cover. He was the star attraction, and many had filed into the stadium early to get good seats.

As part of his ritual preparations, an hour before the race, Santee jogged outside the stadium and then came onto the infield for a few wind sprints. Back in the locker room, he changed and the trainer rubbed him down. Easton was outside watching the two-mile relay, a race Santee normally would have entered. The two had said everything they needed to say to each other the night before. "Let's try to break it," Easton had said. "Do you have any questions?"

"No," Santee replied, and they were done.

After nearly two years of planning and dreaming about

how to run the mile in less than four minutes, there was no new territory to cover.

Fifteen minutes before race time, Santee taped a four-inch square of cotton dipped in Cramer Red Hot analgesic ointment to the base of his spine. It was believed to stimulate the nerves and stir the legs. Then he left the locker room with a towel draped over his head. Underneath, his face was a mask of cool determination.

A bank of dark clouds hung in the sky, and suddenly a torrent of rain erupted. Umbrellas used moments before to shield the sun were now deflecting pelting rain, then hail, from the shower. Gusts of wind blew across the field. Those exposed ducked for cover. As suddenly as the storm came, it passed. The clouds broke, and the sun returned. Short of a few upended umbrellas, everything was just as it had been—except the track, which was covered in puddles and had divots in the cinders from the hail.

Santee was stunned. The track was wrecked, and it seemed that so too were his chances of a fast mile. It was hard not to think that the world was conspiring against him, that nothing was on his side.

Coach Easton went into action. Hands buried deep in his pockets, a sure sign that he meant business, he organized a crew of freshman athletes to shovel off the water. Then he had one of his boys go over the track twice with a power-driven roller to level it off. He also arranged for a propane-fueled flamethrower to further dry out the track.

Santee tried to keep warm as his coach and teammates did everything they could to give him this chance. Of course, he had made sacrifices for his team, but he could see now what friendships he had earned along the way and how much his team supported him.

The track was still heavy underfoot, but the team's efforts had given Santee a shot. He planned on making the most of it. He moved to the starting line, lining up with Oklahoma A&M's Bjorn Bogerud, Drake's Ray McConnell, and Oklahoma's Bruce Drummond, who was the defending champion in the Cunningham Mile. No one in the small field could challenge Santee, and he knew it.

With the crowd already on their feet and shouting his name, he felt charged up. He just needed to stick to the pacing that he and Easton had carefully calculated. First lap: 59 seconds. Second lap: 60 seconds. Third lap: 61 seconds. Fourth lap: Go for it.

Watching from the stands was Danna, Santee's bride-to-be. She had wished him luck before the start of the race and now simply had to hope for the best. These big races were difficult for her. "I just can't talk," she explained. "There's no use trying to be objective, because I can't. I get all tied in knots."

The gun fired, and Santee burst forward. Bogerud started slightly quicker, but by the end of the first turn, Santee took the lead. Bogerud tried to catch up, but there was nothing he could do—and he knew it. By the start of the second lap, Santee was only a half second off pace. Easton was calling out his times, and, despite the cacophony from the stands, Santee heard him. No matter how noisy it was, he always heard his coach.

He was still uneasy. The track was soft and wet in patches, and when he drove forward he lacked traction. There was also a strong crosswind. Nonetheless, he continued to push, extending his fifteen-yard lead. The crowd spurred him forward. In the second lap, he ran a second and a half over pace, and for the half mile he clocked 2:01. It was very good, given the conditions—better than he thought.

He settled into his stride. To keep his arms relaxed, he kept his index finger on his thumb in each hand, making sure not to make a fist. The third lap was slow, much slower than he wanted: 63 seconds. The wind and traction were affecting him more than in the two previous laps. He could still do it. He had run a 55-second final lap before. That would give him a 3:59 mile, and the four-minute mile would be his.

Easton yelled from the side of the track, "Go! Go! Go!" The crowd cheered. Everyone wanted him to be the one.

Santee's training had prepared him for the finishing burst. He increased his arm action, looking to strike the air like one would a punching bag. By the last 100 yards, he was working on sheer emotion and the enthusiasm of the crowd. The timekeepers waited at the finish line. Santee took one last stride, driving with his right leg as he broke through the tape.

It was a remarkable last lap given the conditions. But not remarkable enough: 58.6. The time flashed on the scoreboard: 4:03.1. He had come up short again. The brief downpour had stripped him of confidence in his chances, and the competition was not able to provide the jolt of adrenaline he needed.

At two o'clock the next afternoon, Easter Sunday, Santee and Danna were married in a quiet ceremony in Lawrence. Bill Easton and his wife stood in for Santee's parents, who had not been invited. After the ceremony, a small party was thrown in their honor at a friend's apartment. Their honeymoon lasted less than twenty-four hours. By Monday afternoon Santee was back at the track.

CHAPTER 13

BY MID-APRIL 1954, Bannister felt spent. After four months of the most difficult training he had ever experienced, coupled with the intensity of his last days at St. Mary's before taking the General Medical Council's exam, he really needed a break. Chataway and Brasher were the same. All three were tired and felt as though their efforts on the track, no matter how strenuous, had stopped yielding a return.

Since December 1953 they had improved their lap times from 66 to 61 seconds. But in the past several weeks they hadn't been able to get down to the magical 60-second mark, the point at which they could feel confident that the mile barrier was within range. Each attempt brought failure and each failure a sense that they had reached the limit of what their bodies could do. They tried again and again, but their time never improved. As Brasher said, they were "bogged down."

Bannister had always been afraid that, by overtraining, he would reach a state where more running would only bring worse results and he would be overcome by a sense of listlessness. This was how his hero Jack Lovelock had described the condition of staleness. Its cause was unknown. Some thought it entirely physical: The muscles were worn out and overstrained, incapable of taking any more punishment. Others thought it entirely mental: The mind, tired of willing the body to work hard day after day, could not translate the desire for more speed into action. Whatever the cause, the effects of staleness were very real. An athlete experienced appetite loss and overwhelming physical and mental lethargy.

Franz Stampfl didn't believe that overtraining led to staleness. He wrote, "It is a belief that finds no support in other fields of endeavor. The child learning to write, the pianist who practices for six hours a day, the bricklayer laying bricks—the work of these people does not deteriorate as a result of constant repetition of the same movements." In his view, staleness was the result of having no competition and losing sight of your objective.

Whatever the reason, the three athletes risked sinking into lethargy if they continued to run 61-second laps in their interval training. The Oxford versus AAA meet was fast approaching, and Bannister knew that feeling jaded about his running was no way to approach the task of running a sub-four-minute mile.

Stampfl advised the three to relax by getting away from

training for a few days. Brasher and Bannister went rock climbing in the Scottish Highlands. Chataway preferred to stay and recharge his batteries in the comfort of London. After driving through the night, Brasher, Bannister, and their mutual friend Dr. More arrived on Saturday morning at the Pass of Glencoe, just as day was breaking.

Light began to edge over the horizon, softly at first. Then colors spread across the sky. The thick mist that had settled over the land gave way, and the mountains surrounding them finally appeared. With the windows of the car rolled down, Bannister felt the cool, crisp air on his face and felt renewed.

Brasher and More were experienced climbers, and Bannister was strong and limber enough to handle most of the faces himself. It was stressful, muscle-numbing activity that required the kind of jerking and pulling that his body wasn't used to. A couple of times they ascended routes with mountain streams pouring down on them; water soaked their shirts and spilled out of their trousers, often leaving them frozen to the bone. For three days they climbed, sustained by little more than fish cakes and a few hours of sleep in a local inn while their boots and wool sweaters dried out. There was little time to talk of record miles—or of anything at all except the next day's route.

After three more days' break from the track, on April 22,

the three runners met Stampfl again at the Duke of York's Barracks. After warming up, they ran the first 440 in 56.3 seconds. A very good pace! They jogged around the unmarked cinder track in two minutes and started the next 440, then the next. Bannister ran the tenth lap in exactly the same time in which he had run the first, making the average for the entire session 58.9 seconds. They had knocked two seconds off what had seemed like a wall. It was a moment of exultation after months of training, and it almost felt as good as if they had run the four-minute mile itself.

Later, they gathered at the Lyons Tea Shop in Sloane Square, where they talked quietly of the race to come. Stampfl drew an oval on a scrap of paper to illustrate his plan. "You, Chris"—he looked toward Brasher—"should take the first two laps. Fifty-seven or 58 seconds for the first lap, 60 seconds for the second lap. No faster . . . but no slower, mind you. Can you do that?"

"Yes, I think I can guarantee that," Brasher replied confidently. His speed had improved dramatically under Stampfl's watch.

"And you, Chris"—with this, Stampfl turned toward Chataway—"must take over and complete the third lap also in 60 seconds." Chataway nodded. "And after that it's up to you, Roger," Stampfl said. "You're on your own for the last lap."

It was agreed. The attempt on Thursday, May 6, two weeks away, had the green light.

~

Landy went up the steps of the four-engine Qantas Constellation that would take him from Melbourne to Sydney, where he would make a connection to Singapore, before flying to Helsinki. He was looking forward to his trip to Scandinavia, which promised the best tracks in the world as well as respite from the weight of national expectations. It seemed that he could run 4:02 miles in his sleep but not improve on that time.

At the top of the steps, he turned and smiled for the bank of photographers, and waved down at his father, who had driven him to the airport. His parents' support throughout these many months of training and racing had been unwavering, and his mother's last words to him before he left were simply "Enjoy yourself."

Then he ducked into the airplane and settled back in his seat for the long series of flights ahead. Expectations were still high. The four-minute mile had become bigger than athletics, and Landy's attainment of it was increasingly a matter of Australian pride.

His times since the January meet at Olympic Park had qualified him as the world's strongest miler. On February 11, in Sydney, while suffering from strained ligaments in his left ankle, not to mention battling fifteen-mile-per-hour gusts and a spongy track, he had beaten Denis Johansson with a time of 4:05.6. Two weeks after that, he ran 4:02.6 through semidarkness and a slight rain in Melbourne. On March 5, he clocked 4:05.9. And just the previous week, the day after Santee competed in the Kansas Relays, Landy had made a courageous effort at the mile record on a grass track, despite getting a leather football spike stuck on his right shoe during the first lap. Though his stride was affected by the spike, he tore around the track in a time of 4:02.6.

Whenever he had failed to break the barrier in front of a cheering crowd, it was never held to be his fault. Instead, the Australian press blamed a variety of other factors: the blinding rain, the sweltering heat, the gale-force winds, a loose track, the pathetic competition—and, on occasion, all of the above.

In Landy's mind, if he were capable of running under four minutes, he would already have done so. He hated the thought of continuing to run the same times forever, and if it took traveling to and running on a different continent to have a breakthrough, then so be it. He deserved at least to better Gunder Hägg's world record.

The plan was to spend two and a half months racing in Scandinavia, enjoying the fast tracks and crisp weather, and then to travel to Vancouver for the Empire Games. After that, he had decided, he would call an end to his running career. He hoped Johansson was right when he said that if he could run 4:02 consistently in Australia, he could easily run a couple of seconds faster in Finland and break the record there. It might well be his last chance.

~

In the two weeks before May 6, Bannister trained for speed and nothing else. On April 24, with only a few people watching, he ran a three-quarter-mile time trial with Chris Chataway at Motspur Park. From the start, Bannister took the lead, and throughout the trial he could sense how keenly tuned he was. He felt strong and full of energy. As he described it, "There was no longer any need for my mind to force my limbs to run faster." Every muscle and fiber of his lean six-foot-one frame was attuned to an effortless stride. "It was as if all my muscles were a part of a perfectly tuned machine," he said.

When he crossed the three-quarter-mile mark in three minutes flat, Bannister was delighted. He and Chataway had run an even pace, and he still felt like he had energy left. It was a far cry from his 2:52.9 in July 1952, but he knew how much more strength he had in his legs now—enough to go the full distance of a mile with the same kind of speed. In Bannister's many years of athletics, he had never experienced such freshness and pleasure in his running.

On April 28, he went to the Paddington track at lunch-time for another trial, this one to be run alone. Norris McWhirter met him there with his stopwatch. This was the critical test. If Bannister could get in three laps in just under three minutes, then he felt strongly that he had a 3:59.9 mile in him. If not, if he was over three minutes by even a second, his mile time would probably translate into a 4:01. This was how close to the razor's edge his training had brought him.

The strong wind made Bannister hesitate. He would have preferred the best conditions possible. If he failed to run the first three laps in under three minutes, it might shake his confidence. Finally he decided to go for it, and when he crossed the line and McWhirter stopped his watch, the time showed 2:59.9.

On April 30, Bannister ran a half mile to polish his speed one last time and then he put away his running spikes until the AAA versus Oxford race. He and Stampfl agreed that the best thing he could do now was build up his nervous energy. For the next five days he worried that he was getting sick or that hurricane winds would descend on Oxford on May 6. Only twenty-four hours before the big day, he lost his footing on the polished hospital floor and hobbled around the wards for the remainder of his shift.

Brasher and Chataway spent long hours on the telephone

with him. They let him vent his concerns and tried to reassure him. Of course they had their own worries too. The week before, Stampfl had approached the two of them, over tea at Lyons, about changing the pacesetting for the record attempt at Oxford's Iffley Road track. Instead of Brasher leading for the first two laps, Stampfl thought it better that he try to make it two and a half laps, at which point Chataway would take over to the three-and-a-half-lap mark. This way Bannister would have to take only the final half lap alone, instead of the full 440 yards as originally planned.

They both doubted they were in good enough shape to hold fast through another half lap. However, as Brasher explained, "Stampfl had a way of exorcizing such doubts from the mind of an athlete." Their coach had them so fired up that each runner daydreamed that not only would he manage the extra effort but that he would somehow find a way to kick past Bannister in the final turn and seize the record for himself.

The evening before the Oxford meet, Norris McWhirter was at home in North London, practicing for his role as race announcer. He had spent a hectic day fielding phone calls and making sure that everything was ready for Bannister's attempt, including good media coverage. He had written a story in the May 5 issue of the *Star* headlined "Aim May Be Four Min Mile."

But when he called Peter Dimmock at the BBC, McWhirter learned that the BBC wasn't even planning on attending.

"It's not a very important match, and it's not really international," Dimmock said. "Can't spare the camera or crews."

"Well, I'm just merely warning you that you'd be extremely unwise to miss it," McWhirter said plainly.

"Are you telling me something?"

"I'm not telling you anything really, but if the weather is propitious . . . Bannister is understandably anxious about the priority of Landy and Santee."

"Oh, right," Dimmock replied. He agreed to have someone there for the event and then hung up.

In the bath that evening, McWhirter thought over what he would say if Bannister successfully broke four minutes. He wanted his tone to be measured but his words full of suspense. He decided to start with "Ladies and gentlemen, here is the result of event number nine, the one mile . . ."

CHAPTER 14

ON THURSDAY, MAY 6, Bannister woke in his Earl's Court apartment. He glanced outside, and all hopes of a nice day evaporated. The wind swayed the treetops violently, and the slate-gray clouds promised rain. Distraught, he had no choice but to continue with the day as if the attempt would go ahead, all the while feeling certain that it was hopeless.

At eleven o'clock he went down to the hospital laboratory to grind his spikes and rub them with graphite. Given the likely conditions, this would keep the cinder ash from clumping to the bottoms of his shoes, which might mean a few yards over the course of a mile. He decided to take an early train alone to Oxford so that he could gather his thoughts and come to some resolution with himself about whether the attempt was worth making.

The mile event was not scheduled until six o'clock, which left plenty of time for the weather to change, but Bannister was already leaning toward putting off the attempt. While looking for a seat on the train, he unexpectedly spotted Franz Stampfl sitting in one of the compartments. Bannister pulled the door open, surprised at how glad he was to see his coach.

He hesitated to ask for Stampfl's advice. Even at this critical moment in his athletic career, he disliked the idea of needing to depend on a coach. But as the train sped past warehouses and factory smokestacks under a gloomy sky, and Bannister watched the trees out the window being buffeted by gale-force winds, he finally began to talk.

Stampfl knew the damage that doubt could do to an athlete, and he reassured Bannister that he should make the attempt. "If you forgo this chance, would you ever forgive yourself? Nobody knows what the future holds. Wes Santee or John Landy may do it first. You might pull a muscle. You might fall under a bus. There may never be another opportunity."

Bannister stared out the window as they wound their way across the rolling green hills of the countryside and steeled himself to the realization that, despite the weather, this was his best opportunity. Stampfl had faith in him. His running partners had faith in him. And somewhere, underneath the fear and doubt, he had faith in himself.

When they arrived at Oxford railway station, coach and miler went their separate ways. Bannister's close friend Charles Wenden was waiting for him, and they drove together to Iffley Road so that he could test his spikes on the track. He wanted to see how well the graphite-rubbed spikes entered and released from the sticky ash. Wind blew in gusts across the wet track, and once again Bannister lost hope in the attempt.

Wenden invited him home for lunch with his family, and Bannister accepted, knowing that it would be a good place to relax and get away from his negative thoughts. He was close to the Wendens, having stayed with Charles, his wife, and their two daughters during his postgraduate research, and his friend knew him well enough not to ask him any questions about that afternoon's record attempt.

For several hours Bannister lost himself in the domestic routine, enjoying a lunch of ham salad and prunes with custard and playing with the children. He left the Wendens in the late afternoon to meet Chataway and found his running partner at Magdalen College, reclining by a window, calm and cheerful as ever. The sun had appeared in the sky at last.

Chataway said, "The day could be a lot worse, couldn't it? The forecast says the wind may drop towards evening. Let's not decide until five o'clock." Until that time, Bannister stared out the window, praying the wind would stop rustling through the treetops. When they finally headed down to the track, Bannister bumped into reporter Joseph Binks on the way. "The wind's hopeless," Binks said.

They found Brasher in the wood-paneled changing rooms under the stands. Through the narrow slit of the window Bannister could see the red-crossed flag of St. George over the square tower of St. John the Evangelist Church on Iffley Road. It was whipping strongly in the wind. Stampfl suggested that they not decide anything until closer to race time.

Forty-five minutes before the race was due to start, the three runners went out to the rugby fields adjacent to the track to warm up. While they were jogging on the grass, a bank of dark clouds rolled across the sky, and a rain shower burst over them. The capricious English weather had struck again. They scrambled back to the shelter of the locker room.

Precisely at 5:45 p.m., the clouds cleared, and a rainbow arced in the sky over the church. Stampfl approached the three runners to see whether they would try for the mile record. They took a vote: no (Bannister), neutral (Chataway), and yes (Brasher—always one to say yes to anything).

As it was unlikely they would go ahead, Brasher tracked down Leslie Truelove, the AAA team manager, who was dressed as if he had come straight from a business meeting, to see whether he could switch to the two-mile event. Truelove declined, saying that it was too late.

Five minutes before the start of the race, Stampfl noticed

that the wind was dying down and told the three runners, "There's nothing a man can't do if the spirit's there." Brasher agreed, saying, "We've done all this bloody work, we might as well go." They took a second vote: no (Bannister), yes (Chataway), yes (Brasher). Bannister took another 150-yard warm-up sprint, and then saw the flag over the church go slack. This was the only sign he needed. "Yes," he told Brasher and Chataway. They were going for it.

The crowd of 1,200 was waiting anxiously for the start. In the center infield, two men from the BBC's *Sportsview* program had set up a 35 mm camera. They planned to shoot the race in a continuous take, 360 degrees around.

The six runners approached the starting line for Event No. 9: the mile. Alan Gordon and George Dole, an American theology student, represented the university. Brasher, Chataway, Bannister, and Tom Hulatt represented the AAA. Bannister, wearing a green, gold, and blue striped singlet and the number 41 pinned to his chest, looked down at the track, arms loose by his sides, his right foot slightly forward. He was fourth from the inside, with Chataway directly to his right and Brasher a man away to his left. He readied to spring.

Before the starter gun, Brasher jumped forward—a false start. He received an official warning from the starter, and the runners returned to the line, with Bannister upset that they had wasted valuable seconds of the lull in the wind, which might pick up again at any moment. He took a long breath. His pacesetters were ready. The plan was set. Thanks to his training, he had the endurance and speed to manage the pace. And thanks to Stampfl, he had more than just the knowledge that a sub-four-minute mile could be run—he believed that he was able to do it, no matter the conditions. He was as prepared as he would ever be.

The gun banged, and Brasher shot forward as arranged, quickly passing Dole, who was on the inside lane from the start. Bannister followed closely behind Brasher, and Chataway moved up steadily through the field as they made their way around the turn. Finally, Bannister was free of the thoughts that had plagued him throughout the previous week, free at last to run, and to run fast. His whole body felt electrified, as if he could move around the track without expending any effort. Five days of not running had left him with a surfeit of energy. At last he could put that energy to use.

As they neared the marker for the first half lap, Norris McWhirter read off the time on his stopwatch into the microphone: "Twenty-six . . . twenty-seven . . . twenty-eight." Since he was the race announcer, it was entirely permissible for him to give the half-lap time. This would also help with the pacesetting.

Bannister didn't hear him correctly and felt so fired with energy in that early part of the race that he thought Brasher was setting too slow a pace. In the back straight he yelled, "Faster, Chris! Faster!" Brasher heard the call but refused to react. He was running smartly and believed the pace was right. He maintained his speed, and Bannister, despite remaining anxious over the pace, was forced to hold steady behind him.

Bannister was so restless that he was unaware of how fast he was running. As they reached the end of the first lap, McWhirter's voice boomed out of the loudspeaker: "Fifty-four . . . fifty-five . . . fifty-six . . . fifty-seven." Brasher crossed the line first, Bannister a half second behind him in 57.5, and Chataway third. The three were evenly spaced and already well ahead of the rest of the field. The crowd began to sense that something very special was afoot, given how quickly and purposefully the three runners were striding around the track.

Into the second lap, Brasher sustained the pace. Bannister continued to run on his nerves and had not yet settled into an easy stride. When they turned into the back straight, Stampfl shouted, "Relax! Relax!" Bannister was wasting energy by running so stiffly. Whether consciously or unconsciously, he heard Stampfl and began to get into his rhythm. If they were running too slow, it was too late in the race to adjust. Calm descended over him, and his legs began to move as if on their own. He felt free of exertion.

"One twenty-five . . . one twenty-six . . . one twenty-seven."

Brasher passed the 660-yard mark and began to feel the strain. He was running less easily than the other two and starting to chug around the track like a freight train, arms coming across his chest as he ran. Behind him, Bannister strode smoothly, beating a steady cadence on the cinder track as they approached the half-mile mark. Chataway kept to the strong pace in third position.

"One fifty-six . . . one fifty-seven . . . one fifty-eight."

Around the stadium the crowd started to clap, louder and louder. Athletes in the infield stopped their warm-ups to get to the side of the track for a better view. The time was fast for the half mile, and the officials responsible for making sure everything went according to the rules realized they had a reason to be especially careful.

As they approached the two-and-a-half-lap mark, Brasher was struggling. His mouth was wide open, and he looked ready to fall over at any moment. Bannister sensed that his friend was about to stall and called for Chataway to take over. "Chris," he yelled. Chataway was tired, but hearing Bannister, he found the strength to spring forward. With his short but powerful strides, he quickly overtook Bannister, and then Brasher.

"Two twenty-seven . . . two twenty-eight . . . two twenty-nine."

Rounding the bend, Chataway focused on maintaining their speed, his lips pursed as he ran. Bannister still felt good. He allowed the motion of his arms and legs to almost lull him into a trance. It would be in the final lap that he would have his chance to earn immortality.

"Two fifty-eight . . . two fifty-nine . . . three minutes."

At the sound of the bell for the final lap, Bannister had run a 3:00.4. The crowd had been steadily clapping, with the occasional cheer, but now they got to their feet and let loose. This might very well be it. Chataway made his way around the turn, his flushed cheeks swelling with breath. At 350 yards, Bannister considered bursting past him, but he waited. He needed a 59-second last lap or the attempt would fail. It was too early to begin his finishing kick. Chataway turned into the back straight, his world-class endurance finally giving out.

From the sidelines, Stampfl shouted, "Go all out!" Chataway tried to hold on as long as he could, but then at the 230-yard mark Bannister swept past him on the outside, devouring the track.

"Three twenty-eight . . . three twenty-nine . . . three thirty . . ."

He had to finish the final half lap in less than 30 seconds. He heard the crowd shouting his name, their support urging him forward. His great stride lengthened. He accentuated the drive of his arms to keep balance. As Bannister passed the 1,500-meter mark, his face drained of color and contorted with effort, Ross McWhirter took the time: 3:43, world-record fast. He dashed over to Norris and told him. The twins were convinced that Bannister was about to make history.

At fifty yards from the finish, Bannister had exhausted himself completely. There was no pain; he was simply used up. He forced himself ahead, drawing deep upon a reservoir of will only few people ever discover. Twenty-five yards. Ten yards. Five. He pushed his chest forward and flung himself at the tape, a tortured yet glorious expression of abandon on his face.

When he crossed the finish line, his legs buckled, and he collapsed into the arms of sprinter Nicolas Stacey. Truelove stepped in and draped his arm around him from the other side. The crowd spilled onto the track as the other runners finished their races. After a few steps, Bannister tried to stand again, but his legs gave out. He could barely understand what was going on around him.

"Give him air," someone shouted.

Stampfl moved forward and held Bannister up on his powerful shoulders. Meanwhile, Chataway and Brasher struggled for breath on the grass infield, unable to get to their friend because of the stampede of people surrounding him. Bannister was barely conscious and was overwhelmed with pain. For a moment he could only see in black and white. His system was completely taxed from a lack of oxygen, and his legs and arms felt as if someone was gripping them tightly.

He felt certain that he had broken the barrier, although the time had yet to be announced. Chest swelling with deep breaths, he closed his eyes and rested his forehead in the crook of Stampfl's neck. His coach supported him as they took a few careful steps forward. "Did I do it?" Bannister coughed out, his face still pale.

"I think so," replied Stampfl, concerned for his runner.

Two minutes later, the timekeepers handed Norris McWhirter the official time. It was his responsibility to give the result. Trying to keep his voice from breaking, McWhirter spoke into the microphone. The pandemonium on the track silenced as his voice came over the loudspeakers: "Ladies and gentlemen, here is the result of Event No. 9, the one mile: First, No. 41, R. G. Bannister, of the Amateur Athletic Association and formerly of Exeter and Merton Colleges, with a time which is a new meeting and track record, and which, subject to ratification, will be a new English Native, British National, British All-Comers, European, British Empire and WORLD'S RECORD. The time is THREE—"

The rest of the announcement was drowned out by the joyous cries of the 1,200 people who had just witnessed history. Bannister had run the mile in 3:59.4.

At last the barrier was broken. Bannister finally recovered enough to stand on his own, and he raised his arms over his head in triumph, calling out for Chataway and Brasher. He vigorously shook their hands, his usual reserve replaced by a warm smile. "Without them, I could not have done it," he said to all around him.

"No words could be invented for such supreme happiness," he later wrote. His Helsinki defeat was vindicated, and he had finally achieved a great athletic ambition and entered the history books.

Distance champion Emil Zátopek (#203) running with his characteristic agonized expression as he finishes the last lap of the 10,000-meter race in which he set a new record during the 1948 Olympic Games at Wembley Stadium.

Roger Bannister (#177, far left) runs neck and neck with Josy Barthel (#406) of Luxembourg in the 1,500-meter semifinals of the 1952 Olympic Summer Games in Helsinki, Finland.

Coach Bill Easton holds the stopwatch for Wes Santee in a time trial.

John Landy at home.

Wes Santee at Knights of Columbus Meet, in Madison Square Garden, signing autographs.

Trainer Percy Cerutty.

Franz Stampfl (left), the Austrian-born Oxford University athletics coach, inter-viewed by journalist John Macadam.

Wes Santee wins the 1,500-meter run in 3 minutes and 49.8 seconds, in the National Championships.

Josy Barthel (#406) of Luxembourg flashes across the finish line to win the 1,500-meter run final at Olympic Stadium, in Helsinki, Finland, July 26, 1952.

Chris Brasher (#44) was the pacemaker, along with Chris Chataway, who helped Roger Bannister (#41) break the four-minute mile in 3:59.4.

Roger Bannister breaks the tape as he crosses the finish line to complete the historic four-minute-mile record, Oxfordshire, England, May 6, 1954.

Roger Bannister is hoisted into the air by fellow students at St. Mary's Hospital School on May 7, 1954, in celebration of his becoming the first person to run the mile in under four minutes.

Members of the English team leave Northolt Airport for the Empire Games in Vancouver, B.C. Left to right are: Chris Brasher, Roger Bannister, and Chris Chataway.

Roger Bannister finishing a race during the British Empire Games.

Roger Bannister (#329) and John Landy (#300) competing in a race during the Empire Games.

England's Roger Bannister beating Australia's mile record holder, John Landy, at the Empire Games, running the mile in 3:58.8.

CHAPTER 15

I<small>T WAS A</small> humid afternoon, threatening thunderstorms. Santee was finishing his workout at Memorial Stadium when reporters rushed toward him. He was still sweating and short of breath when he heard what Bannister had done. Instantly he went numb, feeling physically like he did whenever he lost a race.

"What do you think of the news?" one reporter asked.

"I am not exceptionally disappointed," Santee replied. "Of the milers capable of doing it, Bannister is the one I'd just as soon have seen break it. There still is the challenge to see who will be the first American to break the four-minute mile."

"Why were you beaten to the punch?"

"Having to compete for the university, I've had to run everything from soup to nuts. I haven't been permitted to concentrate."

"Would you like to run against Bannister?"

Santee was clear. "Yes, and I think I could beat him if I had the chance."

Once the reporters got their quotes and left, Bill Easton talked with Santee alone. He knew his athlete was stung by the news. "We tried," he said. "But we have to keep on. You still have more running to do."

Santee agreed, although it would be several days before he was convinced of it. More than anything, he wanted a chance to compete against Bannister in a real race, one man against the other without pacing. Then the world would see.

It was Denis Johansson who broke the news to Landy. He arrived at the restaurant in Turku, Finland, where they were meeting, holding a cable in his hand. "Look at this," he said, passing Landy the telegram across the table. Bannister had done it: a 3:59.4 mile.

It was a surprising performance, Landy thought at first. He knew Bannister was about to make another attempt, but he had thought that the English miler would at best break Hägg's record. At least this meant an end to all the talk of the barrier, and he would be able to run without the "four-minute mile" punctuating his every stride. Then the disappointment began to settle over him. After so much sweat and strain, he had been beaten to the record.

Reporters would want his response, Johansson told him. Landy didn't feel up to it. Not now. He asked his friend if he would reply to the cable and then told him, "Well, let's have a go on May 31." He believed he had a good chance, on these beautiful Finnish tracks, of running faster than anyone had before. If Bannister was able to break four minutes, then he felt he should be able to do it as well. He had run many more miles under 4:05 than him—or anyone else, for that matter.

As evening fell on May 7, twenty-four hours after the triumph at Iffley Road, Bannister, Chataway, and Brasher climbed Harrow Hill, west of London. The sun had set, and a cool breeze rustled the leaves in the trees. The three runners looked out on the view: St. Paul's Cathedral in the distance and the twisting shape of the Thames a seam of darkness threading through the glittering cityscape.

None of the three had slept more than a few hours in the past two days. After the race, Bannister had been whisked away for a live television interview at the BBC in London. Later that evening, he met Brasher and Chataway for dinner at Clement Freud's cabaret club over the Royal Court Theatre in Sloane Square. They drank champagne, enjoyed four-minute steaks (appropriately), and danced with their dates. Bannister's was "a tall fair girl in an off-the-shoulder green gown," a *Daily Express* spy reported.

As dawn approached, the previous day's events began to take their toll, and Bannister finally called his celebration to an end. He still had to show up at the hospital that morning and needed at least a couple of hours of sleep beforehand.

When he arrived at St. Mary's in the late morning, he was given a royal welcome. His fellow students paraded him through the front entrance on a chair and showered him with hundreds of telegrams that had been sent to the hospital. Later, he met Brasher and Chataway on top of Harrow Hill, where they had a moment of quiet together.

They had not expected such an uproar. Bannister had won headlines in literally thousands of papers. Together they had achieved the ultimate in sport. But for them it was just that: sport. As amateurs, this race was not supposed to be their defining achievement. There was more to the world and to life than running.

They had so much that they wanted to do: Bannister in medicine, Brasher in business, and Chataway in politics. As Brasher said later of their conversation, "We honestly believed that if you have a dream and you work to make it come true, then you really can change the world. There's just nothing you can't do."

Bannister realized that before he turned to medicine full-time, there was still one thing he needed to prove to himself as an athlete. Since the Helsinki debacle, he had been accused of being incapable of winning a race against the best in the world. Sure, he ran well against the clock, but did he have the ability to win in the heat of competition?

He had to answer this question, not only for his critics but for himself.

Santee felt the clock running down on what remained of his running career. He desperately wanted to run a sub-four-minute mile, and he also wanted the chance to run against Bannister and Landy—perhaps even at the Empire Games in Vancouver, if it could be arranged with the officials. The two milers had been his rivals for too long not to have a final showdown with them. His dream of being the first to break the four-minute barrier had been rudely ended by Bannister's achievement, but he was still hopeful of running a sub-four-minute mile himself—and maybe even beating Bannister's record—at the Compton Invitational in Los Angeles.

On the afternoon of June 5, ten minutes before his race, Santee sat in the locker room at Ramsaur Field. He had already done his warm-up jog and sprints, and Easton was taping up his shoes for him, pulling the strand from the outside, over the spikes, and tight around the instep. This added strength to the arches. "How do you feel? Everything okay?" Easton asked. Santee nodded, quiet as ever before a race. Easton patted him on the shoes and said, "Go get 'em."

It was, for California, a cool afternoon, barely 60 degrees.

In the stands, Danna and her parents were watching him through field glasses. The runners positioned themselves along the line, Santee in the inside lane, his left arm up, right foot back, facing straight ahead. His former high school rival, Billy Tidwell, was also in the lineup, ready to help pace Santee for as long as he could hold on, but they had no strict lap schedule planned out.

They shot from the line, Marty Montgomery of the University of Southern California moving into an early lead in the first lap. Santee stayed back in third position, Russ Bonham just ahead of him. The crowd of 8,000 were quiet. By the end of the first lap, Montgomery had run himself out. Tidwell strode past Santee, then Bonham, then Montgomery, taking the lead a few yards into the second lap.

Santee continued to hold back, having decided with Easton that he would wait until the second half mile before he really took off. Even so, his first lap was run in 58.1 seconds. Pretty quick. As they moved into the back straight, Easton yelled out. "It's not fast enough. Not fast enough." Santee heard him, but he wanted to ride Tidwell out for as long as he possibly could.

By the start of the third lap, having run the first half mile in 1:58.2, Santee knew that he would have to take the lead. Tidwell simply couldn't keep the pace fast enough. As

Santee made his way into the turn, he felt a surge of energy. He was going for the mile record.

The crowd began to chant: "Santee! Santee! Santee!"

Santee stormed around the track. The third lap had always been his most difficult one. Ingvar Ericsson and Bonham were barely clipping at his heels, and it was unlikely they would challenge him. Coming out of the first turn, Santee heard Easton again, "Faster! Faster!" At the bell, Santee was under three minutes by a second.

One more lap. He needed to run it in under 61 seconds. This was the moment to kick, to put aside the pain and give it everything. He was tiring, and each stride was harder than the one before. He could barely hear the crowd now— it felt as if he were running in a tunnel. With only 100 yards to go, he suddenly felt cold. His hands were clammy, and his shoulders seemed to shake. He sensed he was losing feeling in his arms and legs. Still he drove on.

He was long past exhaustion as he neared the tape. His legs continued to drive, almost with a will of their own. This was everything he had. At the finish he pushed his shoulders forward, and the timekeepers punched their stop buttons. Santee continued down the track as he slowed into a jog. His first thought was *Have I done it?*

He turned back to the timekeepers. Easton rushed to

his side. "I think we're close," he said. "We're really close." Finally the crackle of the public-address system quieted down the stands. "Wes Santee has set a new world record in the 1,500 meters with a time of 3:42.8." Easton and his miler shared a look. That was good, but they wanted the mile time. Then the stadium went silent as the announcer came back over the speakers. "Now the mile time: a new stadium record of four minutes and six-tenths of a second."

It was agonizingly close. Six-tenths of a second. Nothing: a flicker of time, an instant faster jump at the start, a slightly more favorable breeze, a half stride, a deeper lean into the tape. It was nothing, but it was everything. Santee waved toward Danna, who came hurrying down to the edge of the track. He hugged and kissed her before he had to turn to the bustle of reporters, eager to know what had happened. He had broken the world record for the 1,500 meter, but true greatness had escaped him in the public eye. He was six-tenths of a second shy.

A few days after the race, Santee received word that the Marines had denied his request for summer leave. He wouldn't get the chance to race against Landy and Bannister.

Since arriving in Scandinavia, Landy had run in four races, but he had yet to find what he needed to break a world record—whether that was in the mile or in any other distance. Like Santee, he didn't have much time left to keep cracking his head against his own four-minute barrier.

There was no better place in the world to train and race. Turku was a quiet old city at the mouth of the Aura River, surrounded by seven hills through which he could run on paths bedded with pine needles and flanked by forest, rivers, and lakes. The air was cool and had an inspiring freshness to it. Here in the hometown of Paavo Nurmi, running was revered, and the city stadium's track was cared for in the way a mother dotes on a beloved child.

When Landy arrived, the black cinder track was dimpled and uneven from the ice that was still frozen underneath, but over the next two weeks the ice melted and the groundsmen got to work rolling and smoothing out the cinders. Landy found it electrifyingly fast, though he had to shorten his stride a little because the bounce from the track tired his legs out more quickly. When he adjusted to the bounce, however, he easily ran 57-second laps, and maintaining his speed required less effort than it did in Australia.

On June 21, the longest day of the year for the Northern Hemisphere and forty-six days after Bannister broke through the barrier that had withstood decades of assault, Landy lined up once again at the starting line. It was seven o'clock in the evening, but the sun was still bright in the sky as he wished his competitors good luck and settled into his lane at the starting line.

He wore white shorts and his Geelong Guild singlet with the number 2 pinned to his chest. Chris Chataway was number 1 in all white, and Johansson was number 3 in all black. Three other milers were also lined up alongside them. The weather was ideal: 70 degrees and no wind. Eight thousand Finnish fans were jammed into the small stadium in Turku, anticipating a great race, particularly from this redheaded Chataway fellow who had served as rabbit for the first four-minute-miler.

As the gun trailed smoke from its barrel, the six runners bolted from the line. Antte Kallio, who started third from the post, quickly angled his way past Chataway toward the inside line. Moving into the first turn, Landy positioned himself a stride behind Kallio's right shoulder, letting him take the lead. He wanted to run as even a pace as possible.

Three-quarters of the way through the first lap, they maintained this position, with Chataway in third place, two strides back, and Johansson in fourth. Landy finished the first lap in 58.5 seconds, Kallio ahead by half a second. He was running smoothly, his form ideal: high knee lift, easy shoulders, balanced center of gravity, heel-to-toe roll as his shoes hit the track. A very different runner from two years before.

At a lap and a half, Landy decided to take the lead. He had waited longer than usual, but Kallio looked to be tiring from such a strong early pace. Landy was decidedly in control, with Chataway ten feet behind him. Kallio, Johansson, and the rest of the field were forgotten. It was a two-man race. Chataway thought that if he held close to Landy, he could dash ahead in the final straight.

At the start of the third lap, the stopwatches registered an average 1:57.9—the ideal pace. Landy thought he had the race in hand. He had been in this position many times, and his competitors always folded by the first turn in the final lap. The third lap was steady and sure. His rhythm was good, and he continued to run relaxed. This was the pause before he gathered the focus and determination he would need to maintain a fast pace through the last lap.

The lead did not change, and the two milers distanced themselves even farther from the field. The crowd was expectant, but they had been here before with Landy. With middle-distance running, the proof was in the final lap. At the bell, the time was impressive: 2:56. Landy was surprised that Chataway was so close behind him at this late stage in the race—only two strides back, which was incredible, given the pace. Nobody had ever been able to keep up with him this far. But if he broke too fast, too soon, he would not have the drive to finish strong. He had seized up around the last turn into the final straight too many times before. Chataway was good, but he had to fail soon. Another 100 yards at most.

When Landy reached the second-to-last turn, three-quarters of a lap from the finish, the indefatigable Chataway was still on his shoulder. This was it, he thought. If he slowed, Chataway would surely pounce. He had to go. He got onto his toes and said to himself, "*Now!*" Five yards and then ten separated them in what seemed a blink of the eye.

It was incredible to Chataway. Bannister had needed him and Brasher to carry him around the track for more than three laps before he made his kick. Landy managed nearly the entire race from the front, and he still had the reserve to drive toward the finish with such speed. It was an amazing display of self-reliance.

Suddenly the crowd realized what was happening. They began chanting, "Landy! Landy! Landy!" Landy was tiring, but he maintained his rhythm as he moved into the last turn heading toward the finish line. The stands boomed his name louder and louder. The timekeepers positioned at the 1,500-meter mark looked at their watches after he passed. It was world-record fast: 3:41.8.

Landy did not hear the crowd or know his time. Having broken away from Chataway, he focused solely on fighting the pain and tension to sustain form. When he broke through the tape, there was no great leap forward. He looked almost as if he planned to continue on down the track. Turning, he saw Chataway finish almost forty yards behind him. He had no idea what he had run. It felt fast, maybe 4:01 or 4:02. Finally the announcer came onto the public-address system and spoke a few words in Finnish. Pandemonium erupted throughout the stadium. Landy didn't understand the words, but he knew he must have done something spectacular to evoke this response.

Johansson angled toward him as the stands emptied and hundreds of cheering Finns surrounded him. "A new world record!" Johansson yelled to him. "3:58!"

Landy was stunned. He had only a moment to register that he had beaten Bannister's time by 1.5 seconds before he was hoisted onto the shoulders of a mass of people and carried forward, nearly horizontal, arms above his head.

He had finally done it.

Eventually the crowd let his feet touch the track again, and Johansson told him that he should run the "Lap of Honor." He found Chataway, who had run his best time of 4:04.4, and asked him to come along. There was no way he could have done it without him, Landy said.

"No, no. It's your achievement," Chataway replied. "It's you they want to see."

Landy threaded his way out of the crowd and began

running slowly around the track, followed by thunderous applause. He watched as the Australian flag was raised over the stadium. After two years of concentrated effort and countless races run well but deemed failures, the mile record was his—and by a staggering margin.

CHAPTER 16

HALF AN HOUR after Landy crossed the finish line, Bannister answered his doorbell. He had been expecting the press, having heard on the radio the report of the 3:58 mile. "Roger, what do you think of Landy's run?" asked one of the journalists crowded at his doorstep, notebook in hand.

"It is a wonderful achievement, and I send Landy my heartiest congratulations," Bannister said. He artfully masked his shock that the Australian had managed to bring down his record by such a decisive degree. He had expected Landy would run under four minutes because of Chataway's presence, but not by two seconds. "Landy had tried so hard, and I am very glad that he has now succeeded. It shows that times can always be broken."

"What next?"

When he had heard the radio announcement, Bannister knew that the race against Landy in August's Empire Games would no longer be just another race. "I look forward very much to racing against Landy in Vancouver," Bannister explained calmly. "But I don't expect that his time will be broken in a race of that kind with twelve men running."

"Will you try to break Landy's record in the near future, then?"

He smiled. "I don't know." When he finally managed to close the door on the reporters, Bannister faced the fact that his greatest race was not six weeks in the past but rather six weeks in the future.

However, beating 3:58 was, if not completely impossible, the least of Bannister's worries. Eight years of study were about to culminate in his final medical exams, and there was a great deal at stake. When he did have the opportunity to participate in races, his results were lackluster at best. At the British Games on June 4 at the White City Stadium, he ran the half mile to Czechoslovakia's Stanislav Jungwirth. The next day, Bannister saw his picture on the front page of newspapers, his jersey spattered with mud while Jungwirth breasted the tape in front of him.

Two days later, he tried to help Chataway claim the two-mile world record and struggled through the second half of the race, finishing sixth. As expected, the British press seized on these failures, particularly against Jungwirth, as evidence that Bannister was better against the clock than man-to-man. Now that Landy had claimed a new world record, a "titanic clash" between the two milers was expected in Vancouver. Bannister started preparing in earnest and strategized about how to run against this miler who had crossed the finish line in 3:58 and, moments later, according to Chataway, looked like he had simply been out for a Sunday afternoon jog.

On Friday, July 23, Bannister knocked on the door of Franz Stampfl's apartment on King's Road and was welcomed inside. Coach and athlete sat together on the couch while Stampfl's wife made a pot of tea in the small adjoining kitchen. Over tea and the rumble of the traffic outside, the two talked strategy. There was no doubt that Landy would maintain a severe pace through the first three laps, leaving Bannister simply too tired to keep within striking distance. If Bannister started his kick at 300 yards out, the typical distance at which he made his move (and there would be only the one opportunity for such a move), he would find it difficult, if not impossible, to keep driving to the finish at that top pace. His best chance then might be to wait, to make sure he never lost contact, and to let Landy draw him around the track until the final turn going into the homestretch.

"That's when the damage must be done," Stampfl told Bannister. "Not before." Coming out of the bend, Bannister should strike, enjoying the brief psychological advantage of passing Landy ("a blow in the stomach," as Stampfl described the effect of being passed) and not giving Landy the chance to make a countermove.

Stampfl assured him that he had the strength and competitive will to "unleash just that extra energy" needed at the end of the race to win—as he had at Iffley Road over two months before. Yes, Landy had run better times with more consistency. Yes, if they had to compete against each other week after week, Landy would probably win more races than he lost. But for this one race, Bannister could summon the mental focus to win.

The effect of Bannister's talk with Stampfl was profound, as it had been the morning of May 6, and he left his coach that afternoon certain that he would win. Perhaps by less than a stride—but a stride was all he needed.

After Landy ran the fastest race of his life, he attended a celebratory party thrown for him in a house on a lake. After a few beers, he left early, surprising Chataway and Johansson. He knew they didn't understand his lack of elation. His 3:58 mile had brought him a strong sense of accomplishment, and he had run it without much strain, but, as he explained, "It was done. Finished. Next thing."

Landy escaped the crush of public attention thanks to Johansson, who arranged for a trip to Naantali, outside Turku, where he could relax and hike along the wooded shoreline. He thought plenty about what his "next thing" would be. The second of his two goals he had set himself to achieve before he retired was to win the mile race in the Empire Games. He knew that now this would be a big deal. As he later described it: "They said you couldn't run four minutes, and there's a guy who does it. Seven weeks later someone betters his time. They're both going to represent their countries . . . It was almost an unbelievable set of circumstances."

In the woods outside Quantico, Virginia, Santee was kneeling in the dirt, fumbling with the straps of his backpack on yet another hike in the hot mid-July sun. His M1 rifle was leaning against a nearby tree. "Candidate," a voice said sternly above him.

Santee looked up to see J. D. Roberts, the former Oklahoma football star, towering above him. Roberts had the stripes of a lieutenant. "Sir, yes, sir," Santee replied.

"We want you to carry that rifle. It's not to be away from your body. You sleep with it. You take it to the latrine. Do you understand?"

"Sir, yes, sir," Santee said, throwing his backpack over his shoulder and grabbing his rifle as the others in his platoon began moving away. He followed quickly behind them, his shirt sticking to his chest after a long afternoon of marching. It was his third week of boot camp, but his first day of training. While the others in his platoon had already been taught how to fire their rifles and pack their gear, Santee had been busy elsewhere.

The past month had been a whirlwind. On June 11, at Memorial Stadium in Los Angeles, he had entered into the final lap of his race with Josy Barthel two strides behind. Three minutes flat had elapsed on the clock, and once again he was in a perfect position to be the first American to run the magic four-minute mile. Then Barthel had surged ahead. Santee knew he needed to maintain an even pace if he was going to run it under four minutes, but he couldn't risk Barthel winning the race. Halfway down the back straight, 220 yards from the finish, he sprang past Barthel like "a shot out of a gun."

The crowd went mad with excitement as Santee decisively retook the lead, but 100 yards from the finish he lost speed. The burst to gain the lead had tied up his legs. He broke the tape in 4:00.7—once again just tenths of a second too slow. After the race, Barthel came up to him. "Why did you go past me? I was setting it up for you." It took Santee a moment to realize what Barthel had just told him, and when he did, he was stunned. The Luxembourg miler had moved past him in the final lap in order to pace him to the finish. If Santee had just hung on to him until the last 100 yards instead of running his legs out on the backstretch, he could have had his record.

Afterward, Santee had very little to say to reporters. It was devastating for him to have come so close for a second time, but he kept that to himself. "I'm leaving my running to the Marines this summer," he told them. "I hope they will let me get away for a few meets, but I certainly don't want to be a coddled athlete."

When he went to the Reserve Officers' Training Corps center to pick up his orders, a major stopped him at the door. "I know you think you're a big hotshot athlete," he said, "but you're going down there to do your basic training. Got that?"

Santee nodded his head. "Yes, sir."

Upon arrival in Quantico, Santee was sent straight to the office of General Clifton Cates, commandant of the Marine Corps School—or "God," as some called the steely-eyed, sixty-one-year-old three-star general who had first distinguished himself at the Battle of Verdun in World War I.

"Nice to meet you, Wes," General Cates said, shaking Santee's hand. "Good to have you here. We're proud to have you as a Marine. Now, next weekend we're having the All Marine Corps track meet at Camp Lejeune in North Carolina. If you represent Quantico, we can win this thing."

"Thank you, sir. But I'm here to do my military training."

"I know, but we have all kinds of Marines coming in for the meet. We can win this thing if you run."

"I need to get my military duty out of the way, sir." Santee looked to his right, where a Marine major was shaking his head violently, indicating that he should say yes or suffer the consequences. "When I left Kansas, I was told that I couldn't do any running down here. What am I supposed to do?"

"Hey, look," the general said calmly. "If I say it's okay . . . it's okay."

An hour later, Santee was in a staff car on his way to North Carolina. He raced in the mile, the half mile, and the relays, winning them all and earning Quantico a first-place trophy. That night he received a phone call from General Cates. "Fine job. By the way, stay down another week, because we're going to host the All-Services Championships."

While Santee was in North Carolina, news of Landy's 3:58 broke, and the press hounded him for a comment. "I'm going to train as hard as I can and sacrifice everything I have to bring the mile record back to the United States," he promised. After his three months' Marine training, he would do intensive, cross-country training mixed with short sprints on the track; in the winter he would race on the indoor circuit to sharpen his speed; and in the spring of 1955 he would be ready.

When Santee returned to basic training, all thoughts of four-minute barriers and mile races were lost to the demands of Quantico. He had to play catch-up and learn how to be a Marine. Lieutenants like J. D. Roberts offered him no special treatment now that General Cates was finished with him.

Two weeks before the Empire Games were due to start, Santee was marching with his platoon when he was told by his commanding officer that he was wanted at company headquarters. A jeep transported him "Mainside," and he was ushered into the office of public affairs. He had no idea what to expect.

The captain got straight to the point. "There's the Bannister and Landy race in Vancouver on August 7th, and NBC wants you to come to New York and do some commentary on it."

This was a cruel request. Santee did not want to watch Landy and Bannister on a monitor and commentate on their race. He wanted to run in it. But because of his Marine obligations, and the AAU international racing ban, he had no choice but to say, "Sir, yes, sir."

CHAPTER 17

AFTER LANDY SET his mile record in Turku, he began training again in earnest for the Empire Games. He had been in racing form since December 1953, a long period to keep at top pitch without a break, but his relentless training kept him going. As for his strategy, there was never really any question of how he would run his race.

Bannister and Landy had diametrically opposed styles. Landy was a "front-runner" who set a breakneck pace from the beginning, leaving his foes choking on his dust, unable to catch up. He relied on pace judgment and superior fitness. Bannister was a "positional runner," who allowed milers like Landy to carry him around the track, making sure to stay close enough that at the bell he could strike with a fast finishing kick. Both styles had advantages and disadvantages, and during the race itself, all decisions about how fast to set the pace, when to break contact, and when to start one's kick had to be made quickly and through a haze of exhaustion.

Most expected that in Vancouver, Landy would take the lead and try to run the legs out from under Bannister. If he set a fast enough pace, Bannister would not have enough power left in the last lap to deliver his kick. But while the Australian was physically tougher, Bannister had the ability to deliver a decisive finish through sheer will alone.

On July 15, Landy's flight arrived in Vancouver, first circling the city of skyscrapers and the crystal-blue waters of English Bay, dotted with yachts, before touching down on the tarmac with a screech. While the plane taxied toward the terminal building, Landy looked out the window and saw a mob of fans, autograph seekers, journalists, and cameramen. Hundreds of them.

Because Landy was proving such an economic boon to the city—ticket sales spiked the day after he ran his sub-four-minute mile and had since sold out—the mayor had come out to welcome him. Finally the police stepped into the melee, escorting Landy to a waiting car, and a motorcycle police escort brought him to the Empire Village, where a press conference was waiting. Everyone wanted to know what Landy thought of his chances in the race now being labeled "the Mile of the Century."

Bannister and a large group of British athletes, including Chataway and Brasher, landed on July 26, and they were greeted by over 1,000 people and a troop of bagpipe players. The press flocked to the main and only attraction: Roger Bannister, now a newly minted doctor.

When they arrived at the University of British Columbia campus, the site of the Empire Village, Bannister and Chataway dropped off their bags and headed to take a swim at the pool specially built for the Empire Games. As they walked past the training track on their way to the pool, Bannister spotted Landy. The two had not met since the Helsinki Games in 1952, yet for nearly two years they had followed each other's every move. It was inevitable that they would speak before their race, and Bannister wanted to get it out of the way.

He and Chataway walked down to the track where Landy was running sprints on the grass, barefoot and wearing only a pair of white shorts. He saw them and came across the field. He was darkly tanned and as fit as any miler Bannister had ever seen.

"Hello, John," Bannister said, feeling awkward.

"Roger," Landy said. He shook his hand vigorously and hardly seemed fazed. Fortunately for Bannister, Chataway was there to ease the tension. He greeted the Australian as an old friend.

"Seen the track at the new Empire Stadium?" Bannister inquired.

"Yes," Landy said. "It looks a bit clayey. If the weather gets hot, it'll get very hard."

The three spoke of the weather (sunny and smashing)

and the arrival of Landy's father to see the race (wonderful), but nothing was said of their upcoming race. "Are you going to have a run tonight?" Landy asked.

"No, we're off for a swim," Bannister said plainly. And after a few more pleasantries, Bannister and Chataway walked off, and Landy continued with his training run. It was the most they would say to each other until after their race two weeks later.

Before they went their separate ways, a couple of *Vancouver Sun* photographers caught the pair of milers in a picture that was splashed across newspapers the following day. The great showdown had begun.

The Vancouver Empire Games opened on July 30 to a parade of athletes, the hoisting of flags, the release of pigeons, and the firing of guns. A far cry from the original vision of unifying Empire countries under the shared principle of sport, the only thing people wanted to read, see, and hear about was the meeting of the two sub-four-minute-milers. An estimated 100 million people were expected to tune in to the "Dream Race" on Saturday, August 7.

Henry Luce, the famed publisher who founded *Time* and *Life*, had sent his best writer and photographer team to cover the race for the inaugural issue of his magazine *Sports Illustrated* and arranged for a plane to be on standby to fly the color pictures of the final to the magazine's printers. NBC took the extreme measure of building a number of permanent radio-relay towers between Vancouver and Seattle to televise the event across the United States and Canada— the Canadian Broadcasting Company, whose first television station had been launched just two years before, had yet to build a coast-to-coast relay. Meanwhile, 560 radio stations in the USA and hundreds of others around the world cleared time slots on their schedules for the broadcast.

The rest of the games was just window dressing. And Landy and Bannister knew it. Hundreds of journalists from over twenty countries followed their every move, whether it was on the track, around the city of Vancouver, or in the Empire Village. Their faces were plastered on posters and newspapers everywhere they went. The media frenzy they had attracted in their home countries prior to this event was child's play in comparison.

Behind a door in the Empire Village, one whose number had been switched to throw off the press, Landy was restless. It was three o'clock on Friday morning, the day before the mile final, and his roommate, high jumper John Vernon, was sleeping easily in the next bed. Landy decided to take a walk outside to get some fresh air and stretch his legs. Given the late hour, he would have the bonus of going undisturbed.

For all his patience with the hoopla surrounding him in these Empire Games, Landy wanted nothing more than to be left alone to concentrate on his contest with Bannister. Advice about how he should run the race had come from every direction. His roommate, Vernon, and Don MacMillan, two friends and athletes he respected greatly, had tried to shake him from his decision to run from the front. If he played a waiting game, they said, he would have a better shot at winning. "Roger's going to sit you . . . and then jump you," MacMillan had said, having competed against Bannister more than any other Australian.

Landy had appreciated the advice, but his answer was clear and shut down further conversation: "I'll run it my way."

Nonetheless, as he stepped off the veranda outside his room, he was nervous about the race. He knew front-running was psychologically more exhausting. Also, he would have to worry about whether he was setting a fast enough pace, and he would only be able to guess at how the others were running. Bannister would be able to hold back and decide when and how fast to make his strike. Until then, his only responsibility would be to stay in contact.

Trying to relax from the weight of these thoughts, Landy was jogging barefoot on the grass when suddenly he felt a sharp stab of pain. He lifted up his left foot to see a gash on his instep. His foot was sliced open, two inches long. There was a broken photographer's flashbulb on the grass. He stumbled back to his room, blood gushing from his foot and leaving a trail of red on the floor.

The light woke up Vernon, who propped himself up in bed.

"I've cut my foot. It's pretty bad." Landy grimaced.

Vernon was as calm as possible, knowing what this could mean. "We'll sort something out."

"We can't tell anybody," Landy said. More than anything, he did not want to give an excuse for Saturday's race if it failed to go as planned. Whether he would be able to run in it at all seemed secondary at that moment. They bandaged the cut as best they could and tried unsuccessfully to get to sleep. A few hours later, as the other athletes began stirring, Don MacMillan came into the room. There was blood smeared on the bedding and the floor. "What the hell is this?" MacMillan asked.

"Nothing, nothing," they both said.

MacMillan was unconvinced.

"He cut his foot," Vernon admitted. "Stepping on a flashbulb."

They decided that the cut had to be looked at by a doctor, but Landy was insistent that it needed to be kept secret. MacMillan and Vernon found a policeman, who arranged for a car to pull up next to a side door so they could avoid the press who were camped outside. They drove to the University of British Columbia health center, where a doctor was sworn to secrecy before being allowed to treat the cut.

The doctor wanted to stitch the diagonal gash, which ran from the instep of Landy's foot to his heel, and he told the miler he would not be able to run. Landy was convinced that because of its location, the cut would not affect his running, and the doctor agreed to tape the gash instead. For the rest of the day, Landy stayed in his room. Several teammates inquired as to why he didn't go down to the track, and Vernon replied that he was resting.

In the afternoon, reporter Andy O'Brien, of the National Film Board of Canada, came to interview Landy as had been arranged. He found a Canadian Mountie posted outside the door, who told him that Landy was sleeping and could not be disturbed. O'Brien returned an hour later and insisted on speaking to Landy. Finally he gained access to the room, and when Landy stepped away from his bed, he left a smear of blood on the floor.

O'Brien asked about the blood.

"I will tell you—on your promise not to tell a soul. Right?"

Landy said. O'Brien nodded. Landy told him what had happened and then said, "I am determined to run. I cannot let down my team and the fans now."

The reporter promised not to publish the news and then left. Landy intended to beat Bannister, gash or no gash. The accident failed to rattle his determination or his confidence.

~

Late in the afternoon on August 6, Santee and his wife drove through the Holland Tunnel and surfaced in Manhattan. This was Danna's first trip to New York City, and as they headed uptown they marveled at the Chrysler Building and the Empire State Building and the bustling sidewalks where the sun seemed to never shine. They got turned around a few times trying to find their hotel but eventually maneuvered onto Park Avenue and stopped in front of the Waldorf Astoria. NBC had arranged a room for them at the hotel, which, at fifty dollars a night, was an extravagance they never could have afforded on their own.

But despite the sense of adventure, it was impossible to escape the feeling that they should not have been there in the first place. Santee wanted to be in Vancouver, preparing for the race of a lifetime. He was certain that he was good enough to beat both Landy and Bannister, and, more than anything in the world, he wished he had been given the chance. The next day, he would have to sit in a studio to commentate on a race that should have been his to win.

~

The night before the race, Bannister was suffering from a chest cold, and he was worried that it would affect his running. Except for participating in his qualifying heat, his days in Vancouver had been a painful waiting game, particularly after he stopped training the previous Sunday. Much of his time was spent in the room he shared with Chris Chataway, who knew his friend was revving himself up for his race and that there was nothing to be said now that would make much of a difference.

With each passing hour, Bannister became more and more fired up to win. He was the underdog in this race, but that was fine with him. In Helsinki he had been favored to win, and that had done nothing to improve his chances. He ran the race over in his head, telling himself that when his muscles told him to stop in the last lap, he would refuse to listen.

CHAPTER 18

THE NEXT MORNING, the sun rose over the snowcapped mountains surrounding Vancouver. Morning strollers walked along the beaches, and the towering Lions Gate suspension bridge began to see the first cars in what would be a busy day for traffic. The weather forecast predicted an afternoon of sunshine and warm temperatures, perfect for the highly anticipated mile race.

On newsstands from Vancouver to New York and from London to Melbourne, the race was front-page news and dominated the sports sections. "Landy, Bannister in Epic Clash at Games Today," read the *Sun-Herald* in Australia. "Mile of the Century at Vancouver Today" was on the *Daily Telegraph* in England. And the *New York Herald Tribune* proclaimed "Landy, Bannister Primed for 'Miracle Mile'."

In newsprint Landy and Bannister were profiled and compared on every score: their birth dates, heights, weights, and fastest half-mile, mile, and two-mile times. Images of the two running were placed next to each other. Last-minute predictions were made. Not surprisingly, the Australian papers tipped Landy to win; the British papers gave Bannister the advantage; and the American press took the middle road, simply saying that this race was the "supreme test" between the two milers.

When Landy woke up, after a surprisingly restful night's sleep, Vernon asked, "How does your foot feel?"

Landy replied, "Fine," but said little else. However, the cut had continued to bleed during the night, and the dressings were soaked with blood. He knew he needed to get it looked at again. The same doctor from the night before told him that he needed stitches, race or no race, and Landy finally relented. After stitching his foot, the doctor insisted that he couldn't run, but Landy was determined. If the cut had been an inch over on his heel or on the ball of his foot, he could not have raced.

When Landy arrived at the stadium, the stands were already filling to their capacity of 35,000. Twenty minutes before the race was to start, he put on his spikes, slipping on his left shoe carefully so as not to disturb the dressings. The doctor who had stitched his foot approached him before he went to warm up, offering him a local anesthetic for the pain, but Landy said he could manage without it.

On the bus from the Empire Village, surrounded by his teammates, Bannister watched the crowds arrive at the stadium, knowing they had all come to see him and Landy.

The past few hours had been almost unbearable for him. He feared coming under the glare of so many people again and knew that as soon as he stepped up to the starting line, he would feel weak and almost unable to stand. He didn't want to endure the agony of willing his body beyond its breaking point.

His cold was less severe than the night before, but he was still tight in his chest, and as he sat in the locker room, with its cement-gray walls and wooden benches, he looked pasty and white. Before leaving for the stadium, he had carefully packed the same track shoes he had worn at Iffley Road on May 6. He had never expected to be running competitively at this point in his life. If he had won in Helsinki, two years before, he would have been happy to hang up his spikes and dedicate himself fully to medicine from that moment on. But the sting from his devastating loss at the Olympics had driven him to continue running and to seek the four-minute mile. When he ran his 3:59.4, he thought that this would have been triumph enough, but Landy did him one better at Turku, and without pacing.

This race today was the climax. He had to win it. Failure would taint his May 6 race and validate the claim that a British newspaper had printed that same morning, telling him that he had "never won a really important race when the others weren't in there to help you." He had to get in there today, spikes flying and elbows pushing, and beat Landy and the rest of the field.

The pressures were much the same as they had been in Helsinki: expectant British public, big crowd, critics waiting to pounce. But Bannister was not the same man. He had a mentor in Stampfl, training partners in Chataway and Brasher, and a more complete understanding of how important it was to have faith in himself.

However, the question remained: How good was Landy? And could he change up a gear at the race's end to fight off Bannister's finishing kick?

A horseshoe-shaped wonder of steel and concrete, the Empire Stadium had been built especially for the 1954 Empire Games. The flags of the twenty-four competing nations lined the streets leading up to its entrance. With the weather forecast predicting an afternoon of sunshine and warm temperatures, it promised to be the perfect setting for the much-anticipated mile race.

Five minutes before the race began, the stands that encircled three sides of the track were packed to capacity. Scalpers were selling tickets for 100 dollars apiece, fire wardens were trying to impose order on the lines still gathered at the gates, and schoolboys were scaling the four ticket booths to try to secure a view of the track.

Everyone's eyes were glued to the athletes as they jogged around the track and began taking off their sweats. The Duke of Edinburgh, who had seen Bannister race in London and Landy in Australia, was present, his arrival announced by a twenty-one-gun salute. He had inspected the Seaforth Highlanders regiment in their crimson jackets, kilts, and high feathered caps while bagpipes played behind him on the infield. Now he was seated in the decorated royal box, ready for the race to begin.

Over in New York City, Santee was staring into the lens of a television camera. Instead of a singlet and spikes, he was dressed in a tan Marine uniform and dress shoes. The race was about to start in Vancouver, and, just like the 1,500-meter Olympic trials in Los Angeles two years before, he was effectively on the sidelines.

He knew well how it was going to be run. Bannister had the faster kick, but Landy could set a brutal pace. If Bannister failed to hang on by the end of the third lap, he was finished. As Santee waited for the transmission from Empire Stadium to appear on the monitor beside him, the race he imagined on the darkened screen included him toeing the line. He felt he had been robbed of an opportunity. The closest he would get to a battle against Bannister and Landy was via radio signal from Vancouver, via Seattle, to New York.

CHAPTER 19

AT LAST THE time had come for the first two, and only, sub-four-minute-milers in history to face off against each other. Two minutes before the scheduled start time of 2:30 p.m., the sun cleared from behind a bank of clouds, and the stands and track of Empire Stadium were bathed in sunlight. It was 72 degrees, with mild humidity, and the faintest of breezes stirred the air.

Landy was the first one ready, walking back and forth on the track, head down, rubbing his deeply tanned arms. His light jog during warm-up proved to him that his foot would be okay, and this improved his confidence. Before the start, he returned to the infield and shook hands with Bannister, who was perspiring and seemed deathly pale as he kicked off his sweatpants. Then Landy stepped back onto the track, focusing himself on the effort ahead.

Bannister was one of the last runners on the track. Tense and anxious to start, he told himself that if Landy went off fast in a 56-second first lap and then ran the next lap in 60 seconds, he was unlikely to have the stamina to finish the next two laps in 60 seconds each. As long as Bannister ran evenly himself, he would conserve enough energy to win.

The eight runners settled in their lanes five yards behind the start. John Landy, in the inside position, wore green shorts and a white singlet. Murray Halberg was next to him, all in black. Richard Ferguson, the Canadian, was in the third lane; the Irishman Victor Milligan in fourth. Roger Bannister had the fifth lane, wearing all white with the emblem of a red rose on his chest. His countrymen, Ian Boyd and David Law, were in the two lanes outside of him, and William Baillie of New Zealand was in the outside lane.

The spectators generated a steady rumble of noise, and cameramen on elevated platforms in the infield directed their lenses at the starting line, ready to broadcast to millions. Hundreds of journalists waited with open notepads and pencils at the ready. The timekeepers readied their new $8,000 Omega watches, which had been checked, double-checked, and verified for accuracy.

Down on the infield, the starter shouted over the crowd: "To your marks!" The eight runners moved forward to the line. Bannister ran his fingers through his hair and glanced toward Landy. Landy shot his own look toward Bannister, then crouched down, facing straight ahead. The surge of adrenaline made any pain in his foot insignificant. Bannister positioned himself at a slight angle toward Landy, standing straight. Nothing else in the world mattered but what he had to do in the next four minutes. It had all come down to this.

A track official raised his arms over his head, signaling for the crowd to quiet down, and a hush fell over the stadium. "Set!" the starter yelled, raising his pistol. Bannister took a deep breath, and bent slightly forward. Landy deepened his crouch, ready to burst ahead. The world waited for the gun.

Its report echoed around the stadium as the milers swept forward, a wave of flying arms and legs all breaking for the inside lane, gun smoke and clay dust trailing in their wake. As they went into the first turn, the burly New Zealander Baillie angled into the lead, his countryman Halberg behind him. Landy was third, Law fourth, and Bannister clawed for room in fifth.

The field remained tight as they moved around the turn, strides lengthening and shortening while they fought for position. Law cut in between Landy and Halberg to move into third position, then into the lead. Bannister stayed a few yards behind Landy, expecting him to take the lead soon. As they approached the 220-yard mark at the end of the back straight, Landy was ready to move ahead of Baillie and Law. He looked like a man impatiently waiting to get through a narrow doorway with two people blocking his way.

The pace wasn't fast enough. At the mark, Don MacMillan, who had arranged with Landy to call out his split times, yelled out "28.9!" and "Three yards behind!" Hearing his time and Bannister's position, Landy increased his tempo, realizing that he had to take the lead and set the pace. He shifted past the two milers as if they were standing still. The crowd gasped as he made his move.

Landy was clearly into his rhythm, his arms and legs moving smoothly as he distanced himself from the field into the home straight of the first lap. Halberg was second, Baillie third, and Bannister fourth. Law, having lost a shoe, slowed almost to a stop.

Bannister didn't want to be trapped behind Baillie or Halberg when they made the first turn of the second lap, so he moved ahead, increasing his speed almost imperceptibly as he passed them. Landy finished the first lap in 58.2 with Bannister five yards and six-tenths of a second behind him. The other runners, including Halberg in third and Ferguson in fourth, looked incapable of keeping the pace that Landy continued to set. Now it was a race between two men.

In the second lap, Landy turned on the heat. For the first quarter of the race he had held back, conserving his strength. Now he meant to stretch his lead yard by yard until he broke Bannister. He didn't want to see Bannister's shadow or hear his breath for the rest of the race. If Bannister was anywhere near him in the final lap, Landy knew he would have trouble holding off the English miler's famous kick.

At the 660-yard mark, Landy, striding purposefully and smoothly, was eight yards ahead of Bannister. In the turn, he picked up even more speed, increasing his lead to ten yards. It was a huge distance. Bannister knew Landy was going too fast for him. A few more yards, and he would lose contact.

The crowd in Empire Stadium began to cheer wildly. Tens of millions of people around the world stopped what they were doing to listen to the race on the radio or watch it on their televisions. Both runners were under two minutes for the first half mile. Landy heard his time called: at this pace he expected to cross the three-quarter-mile mark in 2:58. This was the critical lap for him. He ran hard yet kept his stride economical and relaxed. He had not seen or heard from Bannister but knew he still needed to keep the pressure intense.

Two more minutes of struggle, Bannister told himself, going into the third lap, two more minutes and then it would be over. It would all be over. He was running to his schedule but was far back, and his rival was, amazingly, maintaining his pace. He felt his confidence weaken. What if Landy never slowed and came back to him? What if Landy was capable of a 3:56 or better? Fifteen yards separated them. He needed to be at Landy's shoulder by the last lap, or it was over. Unless he adjusted his speed, unless he relinquished the pace he had planned to run for the one being forced on him by Landy, he would lose.

Into the turn, Bannister increased the tempo of his circular stride, but in such small increments that from the stands it was nearly impossible to notice that he had accelerated. He was like a ball gathering momentum down a hill. First he took one yard from Landy, then two, then three, closing the gap gradually so as not to exert too much energy. His legs ached from the effort, but by the back straight he was only five yards behind.

As they sped into the turn, Bannister felt himself connected again to Landy. He watched the Australian's stride, almost mesmerized by the steady, rhythmic strike of Landy's spikes on the track. In his mind, Bannister had drawn a cord around Landy, and as they moved around the turn he pulled himself closer and closer.

At the bell, Landy clocked 2:58.4, and Bannister was only three-tenths of a second behind him. Ferguson was twenty yards back in third place, followed closely by the rest of the field. But everyone's attention was on the two leaders. The spectators were jumping up and down, shouting themselves hoarse. The race was everything they had expected—and more.

Landy turned into the first bend of the final lap, shooting a glance over his shoulder. He saw Bannister's shadow and heard him breathing. He could only hope that his rival had exhausted himself by drawing back into contention. Now was the moment to crack him. Out of the turn into the back straight, Landy pulled away from him again—one yard, two, three. His shadow lengthened in front of him into the next lane, and he could no longer see Bannister's. As he approached the final 220-yard mark, the noise from the crowd drowned out MacMillan's call, but he could see his Australian teammates gesturing wildly, as if to say, "Keep it going, you've got him."

Bannister should have made his move by now. *Where is it?* Landy thought, looking back yet again. *When is the kick going to come?* He began to lose momentum, knowing he had given everything, hoping it was enough.

Bannister dashed into the final turn, shocked that Landy was still driving so hard. Because he had abandoned his even pace in the third lap, he was more tired at this point than he had expected to be. They had run so fast, for so long. But Bannister knew that he had to win. He had too much to prove, to himself and to others. Every hour of training, every race, every sacrifice, every bit of his love for running had come down to this final moment, this final half lap around the track. When they came out of this bend into the final straight, he had to be close enough to strike.

Once again he drew a bead on Landy's back. Stride by

stride, he closed the gap between them. If Landy had only known how much he had exhausted his competitor, he might have found the strength to go faster, but he didn't. The front-runner never did.

As they neared the home straight, Bannister marshaled his remaining kick. This was his final chance. This was the point in the race he and Stampfl had decided Landy would never anticipate, the strike he had practiced with Chataway. Ninety yards from the tape, he swung his arms high and lengthened his stride, urging his tired muscles into action. The effort took every shred of will and heart he had left. When he passed Landy, he wanted to do it fast.

Coming out of the bend, Landy thought he had finally shaken Bannister—he could no longer see his shadow. A good thing, since Landy knew he had no more strength left in his legs. He looked over his left shoulder to make sure. Exactly at that moment, Bannister hurled himself around Landy on the right in two long strides. He saw the Australian glance the other way and knew the hesitation would cost him, even if it was only the smallest fraction of a second.

At seventy yards to the tape, Bannister seized the lead. It was exhilaration. It was triumph. This was the moment he loved most in running, the moment when his spirit fused with the physical act. Everything was a blur but the finish line. With a last drive off his right foot, he leaped forward, head back in sheer exultation, and broke through the tape. Victory.

A stride and a half past the tape, Bannister's shoulders slackened, and he closed his eyes briefly, as if he wanted to be anywhere else. He seemed close to collapse, and his face was deathly pale. Leslie Truelove, the English team manager, stepped in to keep him from falling.

Landy finished second, five yards behind.

The other runners came in, but they were forgotten. In the stands, stewards kept a feverish crowd from rushing the track.

Landy tried to step clear of the melee, but too many people surrounded him. He had run his hardest, done everything he could, yet Bannister never broke. He gave his well-wishers a smile, but there was little anyone could say to quell his disappointment.

Still held up by his team manager, Bannister drew in several deep breaths. He was surrounded by people—all congratulating him, patting his back, shaking his hand. But there was only one person he wanted to see. When his legs finally regained some strength, he loosened himself from Truelove and, weaving through the mass of bodies, found Landy and threw his arms around him.

"You were colossal, Roger," Landy said with a smile.

"I knew that if I did beat you, it would take everything I had," Bannister said, keeping his left arm around the Australian, knowing the anguish he must have been feeling. Photographers herded around the two, trying to get a shot of them together. Bannister nearly collapsed again, and Landy, looking completely free from fatigue, held him strong.

In the infield, away from the pandemonium, the time-keepers settled on the official times for the top three finishers, Bannister, Landy, and Ferguson, and gave them to the announcer to read over the public-address system. A quiet descended throughout the stands. "Winner of Event 6, the mile: Roger Bannister, in a time of 3:58.8. Second place, John Landy, in a time of 3:59.6. Third place—"

Cheers and applause reverberated around the stadium as Bannister and Landy jogged around the track, waving at the crowd. In the race of the century, a contest between the first two athletes ever to run sub-four-minute miles, both runners had once again crossed the threshold.

In New York, Santee was alight with excitement as he spoke to the camera. "It was a magnificent race, and I think the better man won. Those two boys just threw everything into it, and the result was this greatest of mile races ever run. Bannister was magnificent, but so was Landy."

As the other panelists commented on the race, Santee

looked off wistfully. He felt worn out, as if he had actually run in the race himself. As he later explained, "I was more exhausted because I hadn't been there." Bannister and Landy had both run tremendously, and he would call them later to say so, but he believed that had he been in the thick of the battle, he would have breasted the tape first.

Ten minutes after the race finished, with the crowd starting to calm down, Bannister moved to the winner's stand. He took the top position, Landy to his right, Ferguson to his left. He looked out across the stadium, overwhelmed by the sight of it all. This was his finest moment. He had beaten the best of competitors in John Landy. He had brought glory to his country. He had captured victory in a race greater than any numerical barrier. He had run the perfect mile.

Postscript

ON MAY 28, 1955, Dr. Roger Bannister, now retired from athletics, went to White City Stadium to support Chris Chataway in the British Games mile race. Three runners, including Chataway in second place, finished under four minutes, and Bannister, having lost his world mile record to Landy almost a year before, now found that he no longer laid claim to the fastest mile in Britain.

"Après moi, le déluge," Bannister said in the days after he made history at the Iffley Road track in Oxford, referring to the famous statement popularly attributed to Louis XV. With the barrier mile removed, the flood of sub-fours began. Was Bannister's prediction accurate that because he had removed the psychological obstacle, the four-minute mile might not be impossible? Or had the barrier's fall simply been a matter of progress—of runners training better and more frequently? The answer probably falls somewhere in between, but there is no doubt that the four-minute mile

turned out to be little more than a stepping-stone taken by the fastest milers of today on their way to greatness.

The most recent world mile record was set by Morocco's Hicham El Guerrouj, who delivered a 3:43.13 mile in Rome on July 7, 1999. If Bannister had been in the same race, he would have finished almost a quarter of a lap behind. When El Guerrouj set this time, almost 1,000 individuals had run under four minutes.

So much for a barrier.

This progress begs the question: How fast can the mile be run? If it can be run in less than four minutes, can it be run in less than three and a half? The prognosticators of the past—those who wagered bottles of champagne with Joseph Binks that the four-minute mile was a fantastical dream, those like Brutus Hamilton, who banked their reputations on a "perfect record" that stopped at 4:01.6—have all been proven wrong. As for how far off the mark they were, one has to excuse them for not foreseeing synthetic tracks, high-tech shoe design, two-a-day workouts, engineered diets, high-altitude training, and a field of milers selected from countries far and wide, the very best of whom find a prosperous career and not a little fame in running. This is to say nothing of those who will dare push the body's limits through performance-enhancing drugs, hormone replacement, and—don't be surprised—genetic modification. The only sure bet as to how fast the mile will be run is to acknowledge the wisdom of the old cliché: "Records are made to be broken." The longer a record stands, the surer one can be that some ambitious young kid will put it in his or her sights.

But the methods and reasons for pursuing ever-faster miles have changed over the years. If one is to become an elite athlete today, there is little room for anything else. The best ones train four or five hours a day, and their lives completely revolve around running. When some discover that their times fail to improve no matter what kind or amount of training they undergo, they turn to drugs that not only threaten their expulsion from competition if they are caught but also have dangerous side effects.

Of course, the rewards for being a top-flight runner seem to balance against the sacrifices involved in becoming one. Beyond a desire to be the best, today's runners have many commercial reasons, including sponsorships and prize monies, to claim the fastest mile in the world. But the steady rise of commerce into modern athletics over the years has taken some of the romance out of the mile record. There was more honor in pursuing it for no other reward than knowing one had pushed through the boundary of what was possible.

No matter how far the record falls, people will look back to the breaking of the four-minute barrier and the showdown between Landy and Bannister in Vancouver as two defining moments in the history of the mile—and of sport as well. On May 6, 1954, Roger Bannister, an amateur who trained little more than an hour a day and for whom running was nothing more than a passionate hobby, achieved greatness on a cinder track he had helped to build, in front of a small crowd, a handful of journalists, and a lone camera crew that had to be persuaded to attend. Only three months later, in a modern concrete-and-steel stadium, Landy and Bannister battled each other in a heavily promoted race covered by an army of journalists and camera teams and broadcast to millions of homes worldwide, with their fiercest rival as a commentator. The "Mile of the Century" had all the hall-marks of a professional sporting event except that not one of its competitors earned a penny in the process. If the first race sounded the death knell of amateurism, the second race struck one of the first notes of sport's future.

A half century after these remarkable events, when this author began first researching this story, Wes Santee, John Landy, and Roger Bannister lived only a short distance from where each ran his first fast miles. Walking beside them around the tracks at the University of Kansas, Olympic Park, and Iffley Road, I imagined they must have heard the echoes of the past: the pop of the starter's pistol, the rhythmic strike of steel spikes into cinder, the crescendo of the crowd's cheer, the crackle of the public-address system as everyone hushes for the mile time, wondering whether today would be *the* day.

Our sporting heroes often strike us as ageless. We remember them in their prime, their faces unlined, their bodies still taut with power. If a measure of a person is how he lives his whole life and not simply his youth, then these three men deserve our regard for what they did after their pursuit of the four-minute mile as well.

Wes Santee, who never ran a sub-four mile, had a long and distinguished career serving as a Marine reservist while running his own insurance business. He remained a champion of the University of Kansas and continued to support youth programs in sport until his death in 2010.

After a teaching stint at Geelong Grammar School, John Landy joined the chemical company ICI as a scientist and was head of its rural research and development division by the time he retired. He served on the Melbourne Olympic Committee, chaired a task force to promote Australian athletics, led the Australian Sports Drug Agency, and also wrote a couple of books on natural history. In 2000 he began a six-year term as governor of Victoria and continues to this day to be involved in charity works.

Once retired from athletics, Roger Bannister dedicated himself to medicine, becoming a noted neurologist. He sidelined as an official on Britain's Sports Council, where he led two major campaigns: first, building recreational centers throughout the country; and second, discouraging athletes from taking performance-enhancing drugs, through random testing. In 1975, he was knighted for his many efforts. Bannister also wrote one of the most evocative books on running, *The Four-Minute Mile*, and was the master of Pembroke College at Oxford University. He passed away in 2018, hoping to be remembered as much for his contributions to medicine as to athletics.

During our interviews, Bannister, Landy, and Santee looked back at their competitive running days with a blend of pride and "oh, not that old story again." Santee remained stung by his fight with the AAU. Landy was wistful for what might have been in Vancouver. Bannister still exuded the determination and aggression that gave power to his finishing kick. Dramatic as their efforts were to many millions of people, the three spoke pointedly about what sport gave to them, regardless of four-minute barriers and miracle miles.

Landy said, "Running gave me discipline and self-expression . . . It has all the disappointments, frustrations, lack of success and unexpected success, which all reproduce themselves in the bigger play of life. It teaches you the ability to present under pressure. It teaches you the importance of being enthusiastic, dedicated, focused. All of these are trite statements, but if you actually have to go through these things as a young man, it's very, very important."

Santee agreed. "Hard work pays off," he said. "You have to be just as disciplined to run a business as you do to train for an athletic event. You have to eat right, still have to get up early and work more than others. Great athletes usually spend extra time in the weight room, shoot extra baskets, run extra sprints, whatever. And that whole thing translates into larger life . . . When I'm going to give a speech, like to young Marines, I will plan my whole day around that so I am mentally and physically alert. You can't separate these when you're performing, same as if I was running an event. I still eat my tea, toast, and honey."

And as Bannister came to understand, "sport is about not being wrapped up in cotton wool. Sport is about adapting to the unexpected and being able to modify plans at the last minute. Sport, like all life, is about taking your chances."

Author's Note

When an author sets out to investigate a legend—and there are few stories as legendary in sport as the pursuit of the four-minute mile—it is initially difficult to see the heroes around whom events unfold as true flesh-and-blood individuals. Myth tends to wrap its arms around fact, and memory finds a comfortable groove and stays the course. What makes these individuals so interesting—their doubts, vulnerabilities, and failures—is often airbrushed out and their victories characterized as faits accomplis. But true heroes are never as unalloyed as they first appear (thank goodness). We should admire them all the more for this fact.

Getting past the panegyrics that populate this history has been the real pleasure behind my research. No doubt there have been some very fine articles written about this story, but only by interviewing the principals—Roger Bannister, John Landy, and Wes Santee—and their close friends at the time does one do justice to its depth. Their generosity in this regard has been without measure. These interviews, coupled with contemporaneous newspaper and magazine articles and memoir accounts by several individuals involved in these events, serve as the basis of *The Race of the Century*. With this material, the story almost wrote itself.

I have included a collective reference for those interested in knowing the source behind particular conversations and scenes. No dialogue in this book was manufactured. All dialogue is directly quoted from either a secondary resource or an interview. That said, almost seven decades have passed since this story occurred. On some occasions dialogue was represented as the best recollection of what was probably said. Furthermore, memory has its faults, and in those situations where interview subjects contradicted one another, I almost always went with what the principal recollected. In those instances when contemporaneous sources (mainly newspaper articles) did not correspond with memory, I primarily went with the former, particularly when there were several sources indicating the same facts. Having inhabited this world of paper and interview tapes for two years, I feel I have been a fairly accurate judge of the events as they happened. I hope that I have served the history of these heroes well.

Bibliography

Alexander, Darren. "An Examination of the Victorian Newspapers' Portrayal of John Landy's Attempts at the Four-Minute Mile between 1952 and 1954." Melbourne: La Trobe University, 1991.

Baedeker, Karl. *London and Its Environs: A Handbook for Travellers*, 20th rev. ed. Hamburg: Karl Baedeker, 1951.

Banks, Norman. *The World in My Diary: From Melbourne to Helsinki for the Olympic Games*. London: William Heinemann, 1953.

Bannister, R. G., and D. J. C. Cunningham. "The Effects on the Respiration and Performance during Exercise of Adding Oxygen to the Inspired Air." *Journal of Physiology* 125(1), 1954: 118–37.

Bannister, R. G., D. J. C. Cunningham, and C. G. Douglas. "The Carbon Dioxide Stimulus to Breathing in Severe Exercise." *Journal of Physiology* 125(1), 1954: 90–117.

Bannister, Roger. *The Four-Minute Mile*. Guilford, CT: Globe Pequot Press, 1955.

Brasher, Christopher. *Sportsmen of Our Time*. London: Victor Gollancz, 1962.

Carter, John Marshall, and Arnd Kruger, eds. *Ritual and Record: Sports Records and Quantification in Premodern Societies*. Westport, CT: Greenwood Press, 1990.

Cerutty, Percy. *Sport Is My Life*. London: Stanley Paul, 1966.

Clarke, Ron, and Norman Harris. *The Lonely Breed*. London: Pelham Books, 1967.

Clarke, Ron, ed. *Athletics: The Australian Way*. Melbourne: Lansdowne, 1976.

Denison, Jim, ed. *Bannister and Beyond: The Mystique of the Four-Minute Mile*. Halcottsville, NY: Breakaway Books, 2003.

Gillman, Peter, and Leni Gillman. *"Collar the Lot!" How Britain Interned and Expelled Its Wartime Refugees*. London: Quartet Books, 1980.

Gordon, Harry. *Young Men in a Hurry: The Story of Australia's Fastest Decade*. Melbourne: Lansdowne, 1961.

Guttmann, Allen. *From Ritual to Record: The Nature of Modern Sports*. New York: Columbia University Press, 1978.

Harris, Norman. *The Legend of Lovelock*. London: Nicholas Kaye, 1964.

Hoby, Alan. *One Crowded Hour*. London: Museum Press, 1954.

Kožík, František. *Zátopek the Marathon Victor: A Reportage on the World's Greatest Long-Distance Runner*. Prague: Artia, 1954.

Krise, Raymond, and Bill Squires. *Fast Tracks: The History of Distance Running*. Brattleboro, VT: Stephen Greene Press, 1982.

Ledbrooke, A. W. *Great Moments in Sport*. London: Phoenix House, 1956.

McWhirter, Norris. *Ross: The Story of a Shared Life*. London: Churchill Press, 1976.

Noakes, Tim. *The Lore of Running: Discover the Science and Spirit of Running*. Champaign, IL: Leisure Press, 1991.

The Official Report of the Organizing Committee for the Games of the XV Olympiad, Helsinki 1952. Helsinki: Werner Söderström Osakeyhtiö, 1952.

Patkin, Benzion. *The Dunera Internees*. Stanmore: Cassell Australia, 1979.

Pearson, G. F. D., ed. *Athletics*. Edinburgh: Nelson, 1963.

Robbins, Trevor. *Running into History: A Centenary Profile of the Malvern Harriers Athletic Club*. Malvern: Malvern Harriers, 1996.

Sears, Edward. *Running through the Ages*. London: McFarland, 2001.

Sims, Graem. *Why Die? The Extraordinary Percy Cerutty, "Maker of Champions."* South Melbourne: Lothian Books, 2003.

Smith, George. *All Out for the Mile: A History of the Race, 1864–1955*. London: Forbes Robertson, 1955.

Solomon, Robert. *Great Australian Athletes: Selected Olympians, 1928–1956*. Marrickville: Southwood Press, 2000.

Stampfl, Franz. *Franz Stampfl on Running: Sprint, Middle Distance, and Distance Events.* London: Herbert Jenkins, 1955.

Uren, William T. J. *Australian Olympic Team at Helsinki 1952.* Melbourne: Australian Olympic Federation, 1952.

Wilt, Fred, ed. *How They Train*, Tafnews Press, 1973.

Source Notes

PROLOGUE

"How did he know" Roger Bannister, personal interview.

"seemed so perfectly round" "The Milers," *Sports Illustrated*, June 27, 1994.

Running the mile "Four-Minute Men," *Sports Illustrated*, August 16, 1994.

Running revealed to Landy John Landy, personal interview.

CHAPTER 1

"Bannister had terrific grace" Terry O'Connor, personal interview.

So balanced and even Peter Hildreth, personal interview.

He loved that moment Roger Bannister, *The Four-Minute Mile* (Guilford, CT: Globe Pequot Press, 1955), p. 59.

On reading the time Norris McWhirter, personal interview.

"You could have brought" Chris Chataway, personal interview.

Norris was cross Dr. Ronald Williams, personal interview.

"Roger . . . they put" Dr. Ronald Williams, personal interview.

Roger Bannister was being set up Terry O'Connor, personal interview.

When not on the track Arthur Daley, "Listening to a 4-Minute Miler," *New York Times*, May 14, 1954.

The second child Roger Bannister, American Academy of Achievement interview, October 27, 2000; Bannister, *Four-Minute Mile*, p. 46.

His childhood years Roger Bannister, American Academy of Achievement interview, October 27, 2000.

"I was startled" Bannister, *Four-Minute Mile*, pp. 11–12.

An awkward and serious-minded Bannister, *Four-Minute Mile*, pp. 32–35, 38.

"If there was a moment" BBC, "Suspense: The Four-Minute Mile," July 18, 1954.

A schoolboy among George Smith, *All Out for the Mile: A History of the Race, 1864–1955* (London: Forbes Robertson, 1955), pp. 144–45.

"No manager, no trainer" Bannister, *Four-Minute Mile*, p. 136.

In front of 40,000 "British Miler Beats Wilt; Gehrmann 3D," *Chicago Sunday Tribune*, April 29, 1951.

Tired from all the competition   Bannister, *Four-Minute Mile*, pp. 149–50.

Throughout the winter   Bannister, *Four-Minute Mile*, pp. 153–59.

CHAPTER 2

The roar of applause   Wes Santee, personal interview.

If his father had   Wes Santee, personal interview. Many of the details of Santee's early life were checked against newspaper and magazine articles written about him in the early 1950s.

Easton was convinced   Wes Santee, personal interview; Bill Easton, "Santee's Stride" (n.d.), Archives of William Easton, University of Kansas.

Whitfield advised the young miler   Wes Santee, personal interview.

"I want to make the Olympic"   Jerry Renner, "Wes Santee, KU Track Star," *Daily Kansan*, October 2, 1951.

"Wes, I'm sorry"   Wes Santee, personal interview.

Only the previous week   Dwain Esper, "Four Records Fall in AAU Championships," *Track and Field News*, July 1952.

The coach had the stocky build   James Gunn, "Second Isn't Good Enough: A Day in the Life of Bill Easton," *University of Kansas Alumni Magazine*, May 1959.

CHAPTER 3

Twenty miles outside Helsinki   Norman Banks, *The World in My Diary: From Melbourne to Helsinki for the Olympic Games* (London: William Heinemann, 1953), pp. 54–55.

At fifty-seven, Cerutty   Harry Gordon, *Young Men in a Hurry: The Story of Australia's Fastest Decade* (Melbourne: Lansdowne, 1961), p. 18.

Earlier that evening   J. H. Galli, "Man of the Miracle Mile," *Sport*, August 1954.

In London, he placed second   William T. J. Uren, *Australian Olympic Team at Helsinki 1952* (Melbourne: Australian Olympic Federation, 1952), pp. 58–59.

He even set a new   "Record 2-Mile by John Landy," *Melbourne Herald*, July 1, 1952.

Born on April 12, 1930   John Landy, personal interview; Les Perry, personal interview.

Young John was more interested   John Landy, personal interview.

It was only when he was fourteen   Paul O'Neil, "Duel of the Four-Minute Men," *Sports Illustrated*, August 1954.

In Landy's final year at Geelong   Joseph Galli, "Victorian John Landy May Soon Become Our Greatest Middle-Distance Runner," *Sports Novels*, April 1952.

When he enrolled   Galli, "Victorian John Landy."

The country had a long   Geoff Warren, personal interview.

The two went over to Cerutty   Graem Sims, *Why Die? The Extraordinary Percy Cerutty, "Maker of Champions"* (South Melbourne: Lothian Books, 2003), pp. 100–101; Percy Cerutty, *Sport Is My Life* (London: Stanley Paul, 1966), pp. 34–35.

It took three weeks Robert Solomon, *Great Australian Athletes: Selected Olympians, 1928–1956* (Marrickville: Southwood Press, 2000), p. 163. Solomon has done an extensive study of John Landy's times in this book.

On May 22, 1951 John Landy, personal interview.

In late December 1951 Trevor Robbins, personal interview; Sims, *Why Die?*, pp. 105–10.

"Move your bloody arms" Sims, *Why Die?*, p. 229.

If Landy could Julius Patching, telephone interview.

He was very sensitive Les Perry, personal interview.

CHAPTER 4

Rain from the night *Official Report of the Organizing Committee for the Games of the XV Olympiad, Helsinki 1952* (Helsinki: Werner Söderström Osakeyhtiö, 1952), p. 247.

When Santee woke up Wes Santee, personal interview.

By the day of his qualifying round Wes Santee, personal interview.

Two days later, John Landy John Landy, personal interview.

For the 1,500 meters "Track and Field Prospects: New World's Record Probable in Great 1,500 Meters," Manchester *Guardian*, July 16, 1952.

"There's nothing graceful" Jim Denison, ed., *Bannister and Beyond: The Mystique of the Four-Minute Mile* (Halcottsville, NY: Breakaway Books, 2003), p. 24.

"mad scramble" John Landy, personal interview; "Hot Field," *Melbourne Herald*, July 25, 1952.

He figured there was a lot Geoff Warren, personal interview.

Zátopek fascinated him John Landy, personal interview.

"I shall learn to have a better style" František Kožík, *Zátopek the Marathon Victor: A Reportage on the World's Greatest Long-Distance Runner* (Prague: Artia, 1954), p. 93.

When Roger Bannister made his way Chris Chataway, personal interview; Nicolas Stacey, personal interview; Roger Bannister, personal interview.

The past week had brought Bannister, *Four-Minute Mile*, p. 171.

The others had all finished Bannister, *Four-Minute Mile*, p. 172.

But his legs hurt Bannister, *Four-Minute Mile*, pp. 168–80.

The Duke of Edinburgh arrived A. J. Liebling, "Letter from the Olympics," *New Yorker*, August 9, 1952.

Suddenly they were off Roger Bannister, personal interview; Bannister, *Four-Minute Mile*, pp. 175–80; Chris Chataway, personal interview; R. L. Quercetani, "1,500 Meters," *Track and Field*, August 1952; Christopher Brasher, *Sportsmen of Our Time* (London: Victor Gollancz, 1962), pp. 20–21; Liebling, "Letter from the Olympics"; Douglas Wilson, "Bannister's Gallant Failure," *News of the World*, July 27, 1952; "Bannister Fourth in 1,500 Metres," *Times*, July 28, 1952.

"He is not running as well" "Commentary by Harold Abrahams—1,500 meters," 1952 Helsinki Olympic Games, BBC Sound Archives, July 1952.

CHAPTER 5

Ancient Olympic champions   John Marshall Carter and Arnd Kruger, eds., *Ritual and Record: Sports Records and Quantification in Premodern Societies* (Westport, CT: Greenwood Press, 1990); Allen Guttmann, *From Ritual to Record: The Nature of Modern Sports* (New York: Columbia University Press, 1978). These are two illuminating books about early sporting traditions and how they were recorded and quantified.

Running a mile   Edward Sears, *Running through the Ages* (London: McFarland, 2001), pp. 80–111.

"When we stop this nonsense"   Colonel Strode Jackson, *Collier's*, 1944.

Less than forty-eight hours   Bill Brown, "British Empire Versus U.S.A.," *Athletic Review*, September 1952.

"every time we had stepped"   Wes Santee, personal interview.

Just days after returning   Bob Hurt, "Sure I'll Run the Four-Minute Mile," *Saturday Evening Post*, September 26, 1953.

Having failed to qualify   Sims, *Why Die?*, pp. 136–44; John Landy, personal interview.

On the flight back   John Landy, personal interview; Len McRae, personal interview.

If it were not for a horse   A. W. Ledbrooke, *Great Moments in Sport* (London: Phoenix House, 1956), pp. 39–43.

Not only did he have to read   Brasher, *Sportsmen of Our Time*, p. 16.

Bannister had always thought   Brasher, *Sportsmen of Our Time*, p. 21.

CHAPTER 6

Wearing flat-soled sand shoes   John Landy, personal interview; Steve Hayward, "Mile Star Shows Technique," *Melbourne Herald* (n.d.), from Len McRae's scrapbook; Paul O'Neil, "A Man Conquers Himself," *Sports Illustrated*, May 31, 1956.

Cerutty had promoted   Steve Hayward, "Run Like a Rooster, Says the White Sage," *Melbourne Herald* [n.d.], from Len McRae's scrapbook.

"They don't run on their toes"   *Sporting Globe*, November 19, 1952.

"It's like a car starting"   John Landy, personal interview.

On a typical night   Fred Wilt, ed., *How They Train* (Tafnews Press, 1973), pp. 102–103; John Landy, personal interview; Ron Clarke, ed., *Athletics: The Australian Way* (Melbourne: Lansdowne, 1976), pp. 53–57.

Long after midnight   "Fastest Man in the World," *Sun-Herald*, June 27, 1954.

His resolve was extraordinary   Adrian McGregor, "The Greatest Mile of the Century," *National Times* (Australia), August 18, 1979, p. 14.

Each day, at the University   John Landy, personal interview.

In the history of athletic   Tim Noakes, *The Lore of Running: Discover the Science and Spirit of Running* (Champaign, IL: Leisure Press, 1991), p. 670.

"it's not unusual for an athlete"   Noakes, *Lore of Running*, p. 449.

"Two- and three-mile events"   Ken Moses, "Landy Wins Easily," *Melbourne Argus*, November 17, 1952.

On December 12   John Landy, personal interview; Les Perry, personal interview.

Olympic Park was set   Trevor Robbins, *Running into History: A Centenary Profile of the Malvern Harriers Athletic Club* (Malvern: Malvern Harriers, 1996), pp. 169–71.

By two o'clock   John Landy, personal interview; Les Perry, personal interview.

"Then," he said   John Landy, personal interview.

"Most of the credit"   Ken Moses, "Landy Chasing Records," Melbourne *Argus*, December 15, 1952.

After Landy signed   John Landy, personal interview.

CHAPTER 7

Bannister was stunned   Bannister, *Four-Minute Mile*, p. 184.

"[Landy is] either"   Arthur Daley, "With a Grain of Salt," *New York Times*, December 24, 1952.

In the darkness   Roger Bannister, personal interview.

"Do you think you could"   Norris McWhirter, personal interview; R. G. Bannister, D. J. C. Cunningham, and C. G. Douglas, "The Carbon Dioxide Stimulus to Breathing in Severe Exercise," *Journal of Physiology* 125(1), 1954: 90–117; R. G. Bannister and D. J. C. Cunningham, "The Effects on the Respiration and Performance during Exercise of Adding Oxygen to the Inspired Air," *Journal of Physiology* 125(1), 1954: 118–37; Roger Bannister, personal interview.

"black waves of nausea"   G. F. D. Pearson, ed., *Athletics* (Edinburgh: Nelson, 1963), p. 28.

Afterward, in the laboratory   Bannister, *Four-Minute Mile*, p. 120.

Bannister set himself two goals   Roger Bannister, "How to Run the Mile," *World Sports*, December 1954; A. V. Hill, "Where Is the Limit?" *World Sports*, August 1952.

In 1953, he had a resting   Anthony Carthew, "The Man Who Broke the 4-Minute Mile," *New York Times*, April 19, 1964.

CHAPTER 8

"Coach, let's drop out"   Wes Santee, personal interview.

"Hi ya, ya bum"   Bob Asbille, "Prayed All Year We'd Get Revenge," *Des Moines Tribune*, April 25, 1953.

The previous month, at the Texas   Ed Fite, "Kansas Runners Dominate Relays," United Press, March 28, 1953.

"It was a season-launching"   "Santee Finds Short Race Is His Forte," *New York Herald Tribune*, March 29, 1953.

They were shocked   Wes Santee, personal interview; Dick Wilson, personal interview; Tom Rupp, personal interview; Bob Timmons, personal interview.

"Go get him to run"   Wes Santee, personal interview.

Easton frowned on his athletes Wes Santee, personal interview; Dick Wilson, personal interview; Tom Rupp, personal interview.

"I don't know when" Bob Hurt, "Sure I'll Run the Four-Minute Mile," *Saturday Evening Post*, September 26, 1953.

"I didn't think you acted" Wes Santee, personal interview.

CHAPTER 9

"There are more important" John Landy, personal interview.

"I'll do my best" Ben Kerville, "Landy Lost No Prestige in Missing His Record," Perth *Daily News*, January 28, 1953.

Bannister had raised the money Roger Bannister, personal interview; Norris McWhirter, personal interview; Bannister, *Four-Minute Mile*, pp. 49, 73.

The annual AAA John Disley, personal interview.

He was better suited Chris Chataway, personal interview; Bannister, *Four-Minute Mile*, pp. 192–93.

In the two months Bannister, *Four-Minute Mile*, pp. 192–93.

After an Easter break Bannister, *Four-Minute Mile*, pp. 190–91.

Having consumed Roger Bannister, personal interview.

"to release," he later said Roger Bannister, personal interview.

"Only the silky-striding" Norris McWhirter, "Bannister Runs 4:03.6 for AAA," *Athletics Weekly*, June 1953.

"the four-minute mile" Bannister, *Four-Minute Mile*, p. 193.

"I think Santee will someday" Bill Mayer, "Sport Talk," *Lawrence Journal-World*, June 1 and June 5, 1953; Wes Santee, personal interview.

They made it clear Wes Santee, personal interview.

"I caught my quarters" Norris Anderson, "Santee Sets National Mark in Mile," May 24, 1953, Wes Santee's scrapbook; "Santee Sets Mile Mark as Kansas Wins Title," *New York Herald Tribune*, May 24, 1953.

When Easton and Santee arrived Wes Santee, personal interview.

In the third lap "Oh, That Compton Meet," *Track and Field News*, June 1953; "Fastest American Mile," *Time*, June 15, 1953.

"You guys are crazy" Wes Santee, personal interview.

"He taught me" Maxwell Stiles, "Denis Praises Santee," *Los Angeles Mirror*, June 6, 1953.

CHAPTER 10

Among Melbourne's small Les Perry, personal interview; Geoff Warren, personal interview.

The only time Landy Geoff Warren, personal interview.

"It won't be any good" Joseph Galli, "John Landy Goes into Training," *Track and Field News*, March 1953. The Australian spring is September to November.

Landy never saw his running John Landy, personal interview.

He knew that come his first race "Runners Are Getting Nearer the

Four-Minute Mile," *Sydney Morning Herald*, February 10, 1954; John Landy, personal interview.

"Roger here. Roger Bannister" Don MacMillan, personal interview.

"Santee's going to do" Roger Bannister, personal interview.

On May 23, he had run Smith, *All Out for the Mile*, p. 104.

On the morning of June 27 Smith, *All Out for the Mile*, pp. 105–106; Norris McWhirter, "The Story of Bannister's 4:02," *Athletics World*, July 1953; Don MacMillan, personal interview; Bert Johnson, "Bannister Strikes Again," *Athletic Review*, July 1953. Immense attention was paid to this race, but these four reports are the most authoritative.

"Wide open, Don" Norris McWhirter, "Story of Bannister's 4:02."

"climb the ladder" Don MacMillan, personal interview.

"Maybe I could run" Jesse Abramson, "Views of Sport," *New York Herald Tribune*, July 1, 1953.

"they could not consider" Lloyd Koby of the Amateur Athletic Union, letter to Bill Easton, February 4, 1954, Archives of William Easton, University of Kansas.

"I've run seven races" "Pirie Beats Santee in 4:06.8," *New York Herald Tribune*, August 9, 1953.

In September 1953 Bannister, *Four-Minute Mile*, pp. 203–4; Christopher Brasher, "Christopher Brasher Recalls the Day," *Observer*, May 5, 1974.

The board did not consider "Bannister's Record," Manchester *Guardian*, July 13, 1953. In hindsight, he knew: BBC, "Suspense: Four-Minute Mile," BBC Sound Archives, July 18, 1954.

"It is absolutely necessary" BBC, "The Loneliest Place in the World," BBC Sound Archives, January 1964.

Bannister's failure to break Roger Bannister, American Academy of Achievement interview, October 27, 2000.

The training ground was adjacent Chris Chataway, personal interview; Peter Hildreth, personal interview; Norris McWhirter, personal interview; Terry O'Connor, personal interview.

Stampfl was a talented skier Pat Stampfl, personal interview; Benzion Patkin, *The Dunera Internees* (Stanmore: Cassell Australia, 1979); Merv Lincoln, personal interview; Peter Gillman and Leni Gillman, *"Collar the Lot!" How Britain Interned and Expelled Its Wartime Refugees* (London: Quartet Books, 1980); "The Dunera Internees," Melbourne *Age*, September 8, 1979.

Franz Stampfl was unlike Roger Bannister, personal interview.

CHAPTER 11

"Who do you think you are, mate?" John Landy, personal interview.

From July 21 to September 30 Wilt, *How They Train*, pp. 102–3.

"top condition" Joseph Galli, "Joe Galli Reports," *Track and Field News*, September 1953.

The immense pressure John Landy, personal interview; Jack Dunn, "Timing Error Hampers Landy in Record Mile Try," *Melbourne Sun*, December 7,

1953; "John Landy Runs 4:02 Mile," Melbourne *Age*, December 14, 1953; Jack Dunn, "Landy Could Be Greatest Ever," *Melbourne Sun*, December 14, 1953; "Landy Plans Short Ease Up," Melbourne *Argus*, December 14, 1954.

A cruel gust of wind   Denison, *Bannister and Beyond*, p. 27.

"No one outside of sport"   "Landy: Only 2 More Tries": *Melbourne Herald*, December 14, 1954.

No doubt some   John Landy, personal interview.

"equal pleasure"   John Landy, personal interview.

At the University of Kansas   Wes Santee, personal interview; Dick Wilson, personal interview.

"Look at this!"   Wes Santee, personal interview.

"Wes Santee . . ."   "Santee Spurs Rising Furor over Four-Minute Mile," Associated Press, January 7, 1954.

"The Girl That Finally"   "Wes Santee Sets One-Mile Record," *The Letter from Home*, November 1953.

"I'm really sorry"   Wes Santee, personal interview.

His own outdoor season   "May Ban Whitfield, Santee," *Mirror* (UK), December 15, 1953.

The night before the race   Steve Hayward, "Landy Will Run Hungry," *Melbourne Herald*, January 21, 1954.

Landy's friend Len   John Landy, personal interview; Len McRae, personal interview; Les Perry, personal interview; Peter Banfield, "Landy Goes 'Over,'" Melbourne *Argus*, January 22, 1954.

When Landy took to the track   John Landy, personal interview.

Nobody could keep up   Robbie Morgan-Morris, personal interview.

He couldn't hear his times   John Landy, personal interview.

"master power switch"   Trevor Robbins, personal interview.

When he returned to Malvern East   John Landy, personal interview; Len McRae, personal interview.

The next day, his run   Jack Dunn, "Applause Cost Landy Mile Record," *Melbourne Sun*, January 22, 1954; "14,500 See Landy Just Miss 4 Min," Melbourne *Age*, January 22, 1954; Peter Banfield, "Magnificent Failure," Melbourne *Argus*, January 22, 1954; Steve Hayward, "No Let-Up in Plans," *Melbourne Herald*, January 22, 1954; Joseph Galli, "Landy Below 4:03 Again," *Track and Field News*, January 1954.

"Landy is magnificent"   Steve Hayward, "He May Go to Europe," *Melbourne Herald*, January 22, 1954.

CHAPTER 12

Soon after, Santee told reporters   "Who Needs Foreign Stars," *Los Angeles Times*, March 22, 1954.

"I could do it up to a point"   Wes Santee, personal interview.

Bannister finished his last round   Roger Bannister, personal interview.

Stampfl ran them   Roger Bannister, personal interview; Franz Stampfl, *Franz*

Stampfl on Running: Sprint, Middle Distance, and Distance Events (London: Herbert Jenkins, 1955), pp. 110–11.

"Do it again!" John Disley, personal interview; Pearson, *Athletics*, p. 28.

In Stampfl's opinion Smith, *All Out for the Mile*, p. 112; BBC, "Franz Stampfl," BBC Sound Archives, British Library, 1994; Pat Stampfl, personal interview.

"The great hurdle was" Greenspan, "Bannister's Run Was for All-Time"; BBC, "Franz Stampfl."

After their sessions Chris Chataway, personal interview.

Week after week Bannister, *Four-Minute Mile*, pp. 201–2.

The McWhirter twins Norris McWhirter, personal interview.

greatest double Jack Clowser, "Santee's Relay Efforts," *Track and Field News*, February 1954.

By two o'clock on Saturday Watson, Betty Lou., "The Fleet and Fair"; "Track, Exposition, Parade Included in Relays Weekend," *University Daily Kansan*, April 19, 1954.

Santee tried to keep warm Wes Santee, personal interview.

He moved to the starting line "Santee Enters Cunningham Mile for First Time," *University Daily Kansan*, April 13, 1954.

He just needed to stick Wes Santee, personal interview.

"I just can't talk" Lulu Mae Coe, "Santee's Bride Finds Track Tour Exciting Honeymoon" (n.d., no source), Wes Santee scrapbook.

The gun fired "Next Best Mile," *Kansas City Star*, April 18, 1954; "Santee Decided Too Late for Mark," *Kansas City Star*, April 18, 1954; Dana Leibengood, "Santee Sets Record in Cunningham Mile," *University Daily Kansan*, April 19, 1954; "Santee 4:03.1," Associated Press, April 17, 1954; "Drake Relays Next Target," *New York Herald Tribune*, April 18, 1954.

CHAPTER 13

By mid-April Bannister, *Four-Minute Mile*, pp. 204–5.

Bannister had always been afraid Norman Harris, *The Legend of Lovelock* (London: Nicholas Kaye, 1964), p. 138.

"It is a belief" Stampfl, *Franz Stampfl on Running*, p. 40.

In his view, staleness Stampfl, *Franz Stampfl on Running*, pp. 37–40.

Stampfl advised the three Roger Bannister, personal interview; Chris Chataway, personal interview; Brasher, "Christopher Brasher Recalls the Day."

After driving through the night Bannister, *Four-Minute Mile*, pp. 204–5.

Brasher and More were experienced Bannister, *Four-Minute Mile*, pp. 204–5; Brasher, "Christopher Brasher Recalls the Day"; Christopher Brasher, "Forty Years Ago We Ran into History," *Sunday Times*, May 1, 1994.

After three more days' break Ross McWhirter, "The Long Climb," *Athletics World*, May 1954.

"You, Chris" Brasher, *Sportsmen of Our Time*, p. 11. The exact date of this meeting between the four remains uncertain, but in several sources it was noted to have occurred in April. For continuity's sake, I have placed it after

the achievement of the 10 × 440 intervals under 60 seconds, when it can be assumed that they were discussing exactly how to run the May 6 race.

"Yes, I think I can guarantee that" Frank Bath, "The Loneliest Place in the World—Speaking with Christopher Brasher," BBC Sound Archives, January 1964.

Landy went up the steps "Landy Off with Big Smile," *Melbourne Sun*, April 29, 1954; Bruce Welch, "John Landy at Peak in June," Melbourne *Age*, April 29, 1954; Peter Banfield, "Quest for the Magic Mile," Melbourne *Argus*, August 28, 1954; John Landy, personal interview.

His times since the January meet "US Writer Says Landy Best," Melbourne *Argus*, April 24, 1954.

On February 11 "Duke's Dash to See Landy Win Mile Title," *Sydney Morning Herald*, February 12, 1954.

Two weeks after Peter Banfield, "Landy Romps Home in 4:02.6," Melbourne *Argus*, February 24, 1954.

And just the previous week "Great Run by Landy at Bendigo," Melbourne *Age*, April 20, 1954; John Landy, personal interview.

In Landy's mind Banfield, "Quest for the Magic Mile."

He hoped that Johansson John Landy, personal interview.

In the two weeks before May 6 Bannister, *Four-Minute Mile*, pp. 205–7.

"There was no longer any need" Bannister, *Four-Minute Mile*, p. 206.

"It was as if all my muscles" Bannister, *Four-Minute Mile*, pp. 205–7; Norris McWhirter and Ross McWhirter, "Bannister Does It—3:59.4," *Athletics World*, May 1954.

In Bannister's many years of athletics Bannister, *Four-Minute Mile*, pp. 205–7; McWhirter and McWhirter, "Bannister Does It—3:59.4"; Norris McWhirter, *Ross: The Story of a Shared Life* (London: Churchill Press, 1976), p. 129.

On April 30 Bannister, *Four-Minute Mile*, p. 207; Brasher, *Sportsmen of Our Time*, p. 12.

Brasher and Chataway spent Brasher, "Christopher Brasher Recalls the Day."

The evening before the Oxford meet Norris McWhirter, personal interview; Norris McWhirter, National Centre for Athletics Literature interview, University of Birmingham [n.d.].

CHAPTER 14

He decided to take an early Bannister, *Four-Minute Mile*, p. 208.

Bannister, *Four-Minute Mile*, pp. 210–11; Roger Bannister, personal interview; "Star Man's Diary," *Star*, May 7, 1954.

Stampfl knew the damage Bannister, *Four-Minute Mile*, pp. 208–11.

"The wind's hopeless" Bannister, *Four-Minute Mile*, p. 211.

Forty-five minutes before Ross McWhirter and Norris McWhirter, "The Four-Minute Mile Story," *Athletics World*, May 1954; Brasher, *Sportsmen of Our Time*, pp. 13–14; Alan Hoby, *One Crowded Hour* (London: Museum Press, 1954), p. 125.

The crowd of 1,200 E. D. Lacy, "The Four-Minute Mile," *Athletic Review*, June 1954.

In the center infield Paul Fox, "Sport: Bannister Build-up Begins," *Daily Telegraph*, April 18, 1994.

The six runners approached Bannister, *Four-Minute Mile*, pp. 212–15; McWhirter and McWhirter, "Four-Minute Mile Story"; Brasher, *Sportsmen of Our Time*, pp. 11–16; Hoby, *One Crowded Hour*, pp. 122–41; Brasher, "Christopher Brasher Recalls the Day"; Smith, *All Out for the Mile*, pp. 112–21; "His Day of Days," *Track and Field News*, May 1954; Syd Cox, "Last Minute Decision Led to Bannister's Success," *Oxford Mail*, May 7, 1954; McWhirter, *Ross: Story of a Shared Life*, pp. 130–35; Bud Greenspan, "Bannister's Run Was for All-Time," *Montreal Gazette*, May 8, 1994; Terry O'Connor, personal interview; Roger Bannister, personal interview; Norris McWhirter, personal interview.

"No words could be invented" Bannister, *Four-Minute Mile*, pp. 215–16.

CHAPTER 15

Santee was finishing his workout Wes Santee, personal interview.

"I am not exceptionally disappointed" "Santee Hails Great Run," *Kansas City Star*, May 7, 1954.

"Having to compete" "Santee Lauds Bannister's Performance," *University Daily Kansan*, May 7, 1954.

"We tried" Wes Santee, personal interview.

It was Denis Johansson John Landy, personal interview.

If Bannister was able Denison, *Bannister and Beyond*, p. 27.

As evening fell on May 7 Roger Bannister, personal interview; Karl Baedeker, *London and Its Environs: A Handbook for Travellers*, 20th rev. ed. (Hamburg: Baedeker, 1951), p. 301.

"a tall fair girl" "At Last—The 4-Minute Mile," *Daily Express*, May 7, 1954.

As dawn approached "Star Man's Diary," *Star*, May 7, 1954; Christopher Chataway, "Chris Brasher—Eulogy," provided by Dr. Ronald Williams.

Later, he met Brasher Roger Bannister, personal interview.

They had so much Roger Bannister, personal interview; Chris Chataway, personal interview.

We honestly believed Patrick Collins, "Chris Brasher—1928–2003," *Marathon News*, April 2003.

He desperately wanted Wes Santee, personal interview.

"How do you feel?" Wes Santee, personal interview.

It was, for California Wes Santee, personal interview; "Wes Clips Record for 1,500 Meters," *New York Times*, June 5, 1954; "Santee Runs 4:00.6 Mile," *Chicago Tribune*, June 5, 1954; "Wes Vows to Break 4:00," *Lawrence Daily Journal-World*, June 10, 1954; "Wes Sets 1,500 Meter Mark," *Lawrence Daily Journal-World*, June 5, 1954; "Wind Stops Wes," *Kansas City Star*, June 5, 1954; Ernie Klann, "Valley Sports Corral," *Citizen-News*, June 8, 1954. The account here of this race is drawn from a collection of these sources. Quotes of conversation are directly from my interview with Wes Santee.

Since arriving in Scandinavia Solomon, *Great Australian Athletes*, pp. 179–81.

On June 21 Chris Chataway, personal interview; John Landy, personal interview; R. L. Quercetani, "Landy's Turn—3:58," *Track and Field News*, July 1954; "Butterfly Chaser Runs a Record Mile," *Life*, July 1954; Smith, *All Out for the Mile*, pp. 126–33; "3:58—and I Can Do Better," *Melbourne Herald*, June 22, 1954; "Landy: My Future Is in the Air," *Melbourne Herald*, June 25, 1954.

"A new world record!"   In fact, Landy's time was 3:57.9, but fifths, not tenths, of seconds were accepted in official times, so his time was rounded up to 3:58.

"No, no"   Chris Chataway, personal interview.

CHAPTER 16

Half an hour after Landy   Bannister, *Four-Minute Mile*, p. 224.

"Roger, what do you think"   "Now a 3:58 Mile," *Daily Mirror* (UK), June 22, 1954; "He Sets World Record for 1,500 Meters, Too," *Daily Mail* (UK), June 22, 1954.

When he had heard   Bannister, *Four-Minute Mile*, pp. 224–25.

On Friday, July 23   Bannister, *Four-Minute Mile*, pp. 226–30; Pat Stampfl, personal interview.

There was no doubt that Landy   Stampfl, *Franz Stampfl on Running*, pp. 104–5.

"That's when the damage"   Adrian McGregor, "The Greatest Mile of the Century," *National Times*, August 18, 1979, p. 14.

"a blow in the stomach"   Raymond Krise and Bill Squires, *Fast Tracks: The History of Distance Running* (Brattleboro, VT: Stephen Greene Press, 1982), p. 131.

Stampfl assured him   Bannister, *Four-Minute Mile*, pp. 227–28.

"It was done"   John Landy, personal interview.

Landy escaped the crush   "Landy Rests on Isolated Island," *Sydney Morning Herald*, June 24, 1954.

"They said you couldn't run"   John Landy, personal interview.

In the woods outside Quantico   Wes Santee, personal interview.

On June 11, at Memorial Stadium   "Wes Shy by .7," *Kansas City Times*, June 12, 1954.

"Why did you go past me?"   Wes Santee, personal interview.

"I'm leaving my running"   Charles Stevenson, "Santee Pacer Is Slow," *Kansas City Star*, June 12, 1954.

"I'm going to train as hard"   "Hard Work Basic Ingredient in Santee Bid at Mile Mark," *Lawrence Daily Journal-World*, July 27, 1954.

"There's the Bannister and Landy race"   Wes Santee, personal interview.

CHAPTER 17

After Landy set his mile record   "World Record Schedule," *Track and Field News*, January 1958.

If he set a fast enough pace   John Landy, personal interview.

While the plane taxied   "Police Rescue Landy from Welcoming Mob," *Sydney Morning Herald*, July 16, 1954.

"Hello, John"   "Rivals Happy to See Each Other," Melbourne *Age*, June 26, 1954; "Mile Stars in Guarded Meeting," *Melbourne Herald*, June 27, 1954; Dick Beddoes, "Mile Aces Avoid Talk of Records," *Vancouver Sun*, June 26, 1954.

Henry Luce, the famed publisher   Norris McWhirter, personal interview.

NBC took the extreme measure   "TV Mile Thriller Seen by 40,000,000," *New York Times*, August 8, 1954.

The rest of the games   Arthur Daley, "Dream Race," *New York Times*, August 1, 1954.

Behind a door in the Empire Village   John Landy, personal interview; Geoff Warren, personal interview; John Vernon, personal interview.

"Roger's going to sit you"   Don MacMillan, personal interview.

He knew front-running   O'Neil, "A Man Conquers Himself."

Trying to relax from the weight   John Landy, personal interview; John Vernon, personal interview; Don MacMillan, personal interview; John Fitzgerald, "Landy's Cuts Treated at University Centre," *Melbourne Sun*, August 11, 1954; "Landy Did Not Tell His Father," *Melbourne Sun*, August 12, 1954; "Landy Kept Secret from Father," Melbourne *Age*, August 12, 1954. The exact sequence of events related to Landy's cut foot is not entirely clear. Sources contradict one another, as do interviewees. I have represented the events as accurately as possible.

Late in the afternoon on August 6   Wes Santee, personal interview.

The night before the race   Roger Bannister, personal interview.

Much of his time was spent   Chris Chataway, personal interview; Roger Bannister, personal interview; Bannister, *Four-Minute Mile*, pp. 236–37.

CHAPTER 18

When Landy woke up   John Vernon, personal interview.

After stitching his foot   "Doctor Tells of Injury," Melbourne *Age*, August 12, 1954.

Twenty minutes before the race   John Landy, personal interview; Adrian McGregor, "The Greatest Mile of the Century," *National Times* (Australia), August 18, 1979, p. 18.

On the bus from the Empire Village   Murray Halberg, personal interview; Roger Bannister, personal interview.

He had a mentor in Stampfl   "The Meaning of the Four-Minute Mile," transcript of panel discussion at Grinnell College, April 5, 1984, p. 20.

Five minutes before the race began   "In Their Thousands They Came to Cheer the Miracle Mile," *Vancouver Sun*, August 7, 1954.

The Duke of Edinburgh   "Bannister Beats Landy in 3:58.8 Mile," *New York Herald Tribune*, August 8, 1954.

He knew well how   Wes Santee, personal interview.

The closest he would   "TV Mile Thriller Seen by 40,000,000," *New York Times*, August 8, 1954.

CHAPTER 19

Landy was the first one ready   "Vancouver Race" (video), National Sport Information Centre, August 7, 1954; Smith, *All Out for the Mile*, pp. 136–39.

Bannister took a deep breath   Rex Alston, "British Empire Games—One Mile Race," BBC Video Archives, August 7, 1954; "Four-Minute Men," *Sports Illustrated*, August 16, 1994; Norris McWhirter, "Bannister Slammed in the Clutch," *Athletics Weekly*, August 1954; Erwin Swangard, "Miracle Mile Thrills World," *Vancouver World*, August 9, 1954; Bert Nelson, "Miracle Mile to Bannister," *Track and Field News*, August 1954; Smith, *All Out for the Mile*, pp. 136–39; Bannister, *Four-Minute Mile*, pp. 236–40; NSIC, "Vancouver Race"; Ron Clarke and Norman Harris, *The Lonely Breed* (London: Pelham Books, 1967), pp. 118–23; McGregor, "Greatest Mile of the Century," pp. 13–18; John Landy, personal interview; Roger Bannister, personal interview; Chris Chataway, personal interview. These were the primary sources for this description of the "Mile of the Century" race. I've indicated sources for direct quotes and important specific descriptions as well. In addition, I've used as a model the race sequence described in Harris, *Legend of Lovelock*, pp. 168–74.

"Three yards behind!"   Don MacMillan, personal interview.

Bannister knew Landy was going   Bannister, *Four-Minute Mile*, pp. 238–39.

The crowd in Empire Stadium   Ledbrooke, *Great Moments in Sport*, p. 57.

Two more minutes of struggle   Bannister, *Four-Minute Mile*, pp. 239–40.

"Keep it going, you've got him"   Clarke and Harris, *Lonely Breed*, p. 122.

Where is it?   "Landy to Make Attempt on 2 Miles Record," *Sydney Morning Herald*, August 9, 1954.

"You were colossal, Roger"   "Roger, You're Colossal," Melbourne *Argus*, August 9, 1954.

In the infield   "24 Watches Timed Mile of Century," *New York Times*, August 9, 1954.

"It was a magnificent race"   "Santee Says Thrilling," *Daily Mail* (UK), August 9, 1954.

"I was more exhausted"   Wes Santee, personal interview.

Photograph and Illustration Credits

Index

Page numbers followed by *p* indicate photos.

Acknowledgments

When beginning to research Bannister's four-minute mile triumph, I was inspired by the words of Alan Hoby, who in 1954 documented the role of a good sportswriter:

"It is not simply to write a technical treatise in which the performer is dissected like some laboratory specimen . . . It is much more. It is heat and fire, drama and high excitement. It is victory and disaster. It is perspiration and the pungent whiff of liniment. It is the roar of the crowd . . . Above all, it is recapturing for the reader the supreme effort of the [athlete]—the very heartbeats of the particular triumph or tragedy the reporter is striving to word-paint."

Re-creating the events of a story that occurred many decades before in this manner is no small feat, and any success I have had is thanks to the patience and forthrightness of Roger Bannister, John Landy, and Wes Santee. They each sat through several interview sessions, responded to scores of questions, and then entertained follow-up phone calls and correspondence providing further detail. I never could have written this book without them, and they have my heartfelt appreciation and respect.

In my travels to visit each of the principals I also connected with their friends, running mates, and acquaintances from the time, many of whom invited me into their homes and discussed days past. Thank you to Chris Chataway, Norris McWhirter, Nicolas Stacey, Ronald Williams, John Disley, Peter Hildreth, Terry O'Connor, and Pat Stampfl for regaling me with stories of Roger Bannister. Thank you to Len McRae, Geoff Warren, Trevor Robbins, John Vernon, Don Macmillan, Les Perry, Julius Patching, Ron Clarke, Robbie Morgan-Morris, Merv Lincoln, Kev Dynan, and Murray Halberg for sharing their recollections of John Landy. And thank you to Tom Rupp, Dick Wilson, Al Frame, Lloyd Koby, Bob Timmons, Bill Mayer, Don Humphreys, and Herbie Semper for their many helpful insights and anecdotes about Wes Santee.

I would like to thank my publishing team. First my literary agent, Eric Lupfer, who fulfilled my ambition to see Bannister's story told to a young adult audience. Second, Liz Hudson, doyenne of the written word, who helped craft this book from start to finish. And finally to my editor Lisa Sandell and the whole Scholastic crew, who continue to support and believe in my work. Thank you all.

And as always to my family, especially my eldest daughter, Charlotte, whose involvement in cross-country running (go high school state champs!) inspired me to start this book in the first place.

About the Author

Neal Bascomb is the author of *The Nazi Hunters*, winner of the YALSA Excellence in Nonfiction Award, among numerous other awards. *School Library Journal* called his second young adult book, *Sabotage*, "excellent" in a starred review and *The Grand Escape* a "fantastic pick for avid history readers," also in a starred review. Of his *BCCB* Blue Ribbon Best Book, *The Racers*, *Booklist* wrote in a starred review that "this book will enthrall."

Neal is also the author of nine nonfiction books for adults on subjects ranging from a 1905 Russian submarine mutiny to a contemporary high school robotics team. *The Perfect Mile*, of which this book is an adaptation, *Winter Fortress*, and *Hunting Eichmann* all went on to be *New York Times* and international bestsellers.

He lives in Philadelphia with his family and rascal dog, Moses. Please visit his website at nealbascomb.com and follow him on Facebook at @nealrbascomb.